HERE'S WHAT THE CRITICS SAY

about *How to Write*

Superb!—**William Safire,** *The New York Times*

Reading *How to Write* is like discovering the trick behind a magic act. Once the act is understood, it isn't nearly as awesome as it had seemed. It becomes almost easy to learn and execute. *How to Write* can be read in less than an hour and should be kept thereafter between the dictionary and the thesaurus.
> —**Harriet Gerard,** Hearst Feature Service

Seamless, clear prose is what *How to Write* is about. Like Strunk's classic, *Elements of Style*, and Fowler's masterful volume, *The King's English*, the Meyer book is about common sense.
> —**Wesley Pruden,** *The Washington Times*

A helpful handbook for all writers.—**Scouting**

The writing book anyone can use...Refreshingly useful, *How to Write* is the most affordable fast-read yet on the subject.
> —**Training and Development Journal**

This little book is one of the more helpful guides for the beginning writer. It emphasizes good organization in getting started on a first draft, and gives clear, intelligent counsel on how to do this...Will surely help the young, the confused, and the struggling.
> —**The Washington Post**

Shows would-be writers -- from high-school-age up -- how any writing task is a matter of organizing for the job, turning out a first draft, and polishing the product.—**NEA Today**

It is hard to imagine a more practical how-to book on the subject of writing than the one turned out by this husband and wife team. The Meyers provide numerous clear and detailed guidelines that will be a godsend to the novice struggling with his/her first writing project, as well as a welcome aid to the more seasoned writer occasionally floundering about for just the right technique to develop an idea.
> —**Voice of Youth Advocates**

How to Write

Communicating Ideas and Information

Herbert and Jill Meyer

Storm King Press

Friday Harbor, Washington

Storm King Press books are available at special discounts for
bulk purchases for sales, promotions, premiums, fund rais-
ing or non-profit educational use. Special editions or book
excerpts can also be created to specifications. For details
contact:

Storm King Press
P.O. Box 2089
Friday Harbor, Washington 98250

Tel: (206) 378-3910

Manufactured in the United States

ISBN: 0-935166-07-6

For Tom and Anna

Table of Contents

Introduction

We are in the midst of a writing revolution. The combination of today's computers and the word processing software they run has virtually eliminated the physical drudgery of creating text. It is easier now than ever before to type, to insert, to delete, to cut-and-paste, to edit, and to format text. And today's telecommunications technology has accelerated the distribution of written material. We can send notes, letters, memos, reports and articles around the world literally at the speed of light. We have fax machines in our offices, in our homes, even in our cars. With electronic mail systems and electronic bulletin boards we can post messages to our colleagues, our friends and to people anywhere on earth we have never met but who share common interests with us.

The result of this revolution is an exponential increase —an explosion, really—in the total volume of new text being created. Today more people are communicating more ideas, and more information, than ever before in history. The average person absorbs more information in a year than his or her grandfather would have absorbed in his entire life. And the torrent of information pouring over us today is but a trickle compared to what lies ahead in years to come.

All this has intensified the competition for each reader's time and attention. Because there is so much to read, and too little time in which to read all of it, readers are being forced to become more selective. First, they make instant decisions about about what to read from the unending flow that reaches them; which pieces of writing to focus on and which to ignore. Second, after choosing which pieces of writing to read, they spend less time with each piece than they would like to spend with it were they not so busy.

This means that the ability to write well—to communicate your ideas and your information clearly and concisely—no longer is merely desirable. It is critical. When lack of time forces readers to choose, they tend to reject those pieces of writing that at first glance appear to be wordy, poorly thought out, badly organized, generally difficult to understand. And even for those pieces that survive this first cut, the reader's time and attention are limited.

A piece of writing gets one shot. If the reader cannot easily and quickly figure out whatever the writer is trying to say, that piece of writing gets set aside *regardless of the knowledge that may lie within it*—then buried forever in the unending flow of new information. No longer can a writer count on his or her reader taking sufficient time to read, then digest the piece; to sit quietly, to think about it, perhaps to re-read some or all of it, in short to devote the intellectual effort required to discern what the writer is driving at. If the reader doesn't get the writer's point—and get it fast—the reader moves on to the next piece in the pile.

As yet there is no hardware or software product capable of producing clear and concise writing. There may never be such a product. For this is fundamentally a "wetware" task, which means the work must be done inside the writer's brain. More than ever before, a writer must help his or her reader by making that reader's job easier—by writing so clearly, and so concisely, that with the least possible effort the reader can understand whatever the writer is trying to say.

How to Write is designed to improve your "wetware". It will do this by teaching you the skills and techniques of communicating ideas and information clearly and concisely. In this New Edition we have preserved the format of the original book, and of course much of its content. But we have updated examples as appropriate, and generally made whatever changes we deemed useful now that just about everyone who writes does so on a computer.

By reading our book you will, so to speak, install the *How to Write* program onto your "wet drive"—your brain —so that when you sit down to write you can boot up the intellectual skills and techniques of communicating ideas and information. By doing so you will be able to make the best possible use of the remarkable hardware and software now available, and of the even more remarkable hardware and software that scientists and technicians are dreaming of and creating for us right now.

How to Use This Book

Let's begin by setting aside a myth: that the way to write is to sit for hours on end at a desk or kitchen table, staring at a blank computer screen and waiting patiently—sometimes desperately—for inspiration to strike.

Nonsense. In real life it never happens this way. Never. Not even for the best and most successful professional writers. It only looks this way because the key decisions a writer needs to make, and the steps that he or she then must take to turn these decisions into words, sentences, paragraphs, pages, and so forth, are invisible to people who haven't been shown what these decisions are and how to take the various steps that follow.

In fact, writing is less of an art than a process. And like any process, this one involves a series of decisions and steps that, when done in the correct order and with reasonable attention to detail, just about guarantee a decent and acceptable result. Happily, it isn't very difficult to make these key decisions and steps that the writing process requires. And neither is it all that hard to take the steps that turn these decisions into polished, finished prose.

The trick to writing lies in knowing what these decisions are, recognizing just what steps these decisions will require you to take next, and mastering the techniques and procedures to do it all efficiently.

This handbook is designed to help you write by showing you first, the key decisions and steps all writers need to make and, second, the skills and techniques that will turn these decisions and steps into finished, polished prose. In other words, this handbook is designed to show you how to write. For regardless of what language you speak, and regardless of what it is you are writing—a report, a letter, a memo, an essay, a book, or whatever—the writing process is always the same. Without a grasp of this process, you will have trouble writing anything, in any language; with a grasp of this process, you will be able to write anything you need or want to write, in whatever language you speak. This handbook is designed for everyone who needs or wants to write, including business executives, lawyers, doctors, administrators, managers, scientists, engineers, technicians, and students at all levels. It is designed to help those of you who become paralyzed by the very thought of writing, those of you who write easily but are unable to focus what you write so that your readers can grasp your point, and those of you who struggle along every time out, wondering why what ought to be a simple writing job always drains so much time and energy.

Like the writing process itself, this book is divided into three parts:

- Organizing for the Job
- Turning Out a Draft
- Polishing the Product

It doesn't matter what you are writing. You always work your way through all three parts, and you always do it in the same order. Of course, if you're writing something short and simple like a thank-you note for a birthday gift, you won't need to spend a lot of time organizing for the job. However, you will likely to need spend much if not most of your time looking for just the right words to express your gratitude, which is to say turning out a first draft and then polishing the product. On the other hand, should you be writing, say, a history of World War I, organizing for the job could take years. Indeed, it could take longer to organize—that is, to do your research—than to turn out a draft and then polish the product.

Moreover, different writers have different strengths and weaknesses. Some people are especially good organizers; their problem is turning what they've organized into whole sentences and paragraphs that capture what they have learned. Other people organize badly but write well; when these people sit down to turn out a first draft, the words flow smoothly but they find they just can't focus their thoughts in a way that makes these thoughts comprehensible to anyone else. And still others always manage to turn out so-so drafts, but can't figure out how to complete the job. So different writers need to spend different percentages of their time and effort on the three parts of the writing process. The point to keep in mind is that whatever your writing project—and whatever your personal strengths and weaknesses—you will need to perform all three parts, in the correct order, to write efficiently and effectively.

Part One of *How to Write* will show you how to organize for virtually any writing project. Part Two will show how to turn the material you have organized into a first draft. And Part Three will show how to turn that draft into a polished, ready-to-go piece of writing.

To use this book effectively, read it through once from cover to cover. This will take about an hour. You don't need to memorize anything at all. Your goal is to become familiar with the three parts, and the key steps within each part, that all together comprise the process of writing. You want to begin thinking about writing not as a mystical art form that depends utterly on born talent or inspiration, but rather as a series of decisions, steps, and techniques that you can master and whose final result will be the clear, successful product you want.

Your real use of *How to Write* will come when you need to begin an actual project. Remember, this is a handbook. So keep it handy. Use it to guide yourself from start to finish through your own project. When you begin an actual project, read through Part One again and apply its decisions, steps, and techniques to whatever you are writing. Only when you feel that you have successfully organized for the job at hand should you go on to Part Two. Likewise, only when you have turned out an acceptable first draft, based on the decisions, steps, and techniques outlined in Part Two of *How to Write*, should you go on to Part Three.

Again, keep in mind that writing is a process. As with any process, when you are just getting started its various decisions, steps and techniques always appear to be more difficult and complicated than they really are. And, as with any process, you can be sure that this one will become much easier with experience. Eventually the various decisions, steps and techniques will become second nature. So don't become discouraged if at first it all seems a bit difficult and complicated. After a while it will all become natural—well, almost natural—and writing itself will be much, much easier than you ever imagined it could be.

PART ONE

Organizing
for the Job

Knowing how to organize for the job—for any job—is what separates the amateurs from the professionals. That's because organizing for a job is the least visible part of any process, and therefore the one that most amateurs don't know and, all too often, are not even aware exists. It's the part of a process that, when learned, usually leaves an amateur shaking his or her head ruefully while saying something like, "Oh, so that's how they do it."

On the other hand, a professional understands not only the need to organize properly for whatever job he or she plans to do, but also how to organize for that job. It makes no difference what the job is; you have to organize for it if you are going to do it properly. For instance, if you're going to paint a room you don't just run out to a hardware store, buy a brush and a bucket of paint, then run back home and start slapping the stuff on your walls. First you take down whatever pictures and curtains may be hanging, move your furniture to the center of the room, cover it up, and perhaps put masking tape around the window edges to keep paint from getting onto the glass. All this is organizing for the job, and if you have ever painted a room without organizing properly you know what a mess it can turn out to be. Likewise with baking a cake or bathing a baby; either you organize properly or you stumble your way through the process, wasting time and energy all the while and some-how never quite winding up how and where you want to be.

When you set out to write something—anything—organizing for the job is as every bit as crucial as it is for any other process. Moreover, for reasons we simply cannot understand this part of the writing process generally receives the least amount of attention in schools and in writing textbooks. Some schools and textbooks don't teach orga-nizing-for-the-job-of-writing at all. So don't be worried or upset if what follows in this section of *How to Write* seems new and, at first, a bit odd. You'll master it quickly enough because it's really not that hard. In fact, it isn't hard at all. And when you have mastered the techniques of organizing-for-the-job-of-writing, don't be surprised to find yourself shaking your head ruefully and saying, "Oh, so that's how they do it."

As you will see in the steps that follow, organizing-for-the-job is primarily a thinking, list-making, and gathering-up process, during which you will need to:

1. *Choose your category,*
2. *Pick your points,*
3. *Collect your details.*

STEP ONE—Choosing Your Category:

The first step you need to take when you launch a writing project is so basic, and so obvious, that most people don't even realize that this step needs to be taken: You have to decide what it is you are going to write.

After all, every single piece of writing ever written fits into one or another category. There are literally dozens of categories, most of which you are already familiar with even though you may never actually have thought about it. For instance, there are press releases, articles for professional or trade journals, essays, books reviews, newspaper articles, advertisements, sales proposals, sales brochures, progress reports, reports of meetings, memos, letters of complaint, poems, novels, history textbooks, and so forth. To cite one rather obvious example, the item you are looking at this very moment is a "how-to" book, which is itself a very special and distinct category of writing.

It is important to recognize that all pieces of writing fit into one or another category, because each category has its own requirements, its own format, in short its own unique "look". Read through any ten sales proposals, and you will discover that no matter how different they are—no matter how different the products or services they are trying to sell

—the similarities among the ten proposals are more striking than the differences. Each will refer to a product or service, each will articulate the advantages of this product or service to the proposed customer, and each will provide some basic information about the product or service such as cost, size, and so forth. Likewise, all book reviews—no matter what the book being reviewed, no matter what language the review is written in—provide the book's title, author, and publisher. All describe the book under review, and all give some idea of the reviewer's opinion.

By deciding what you are going to write, you begin to focus on the requirements and format of your finished product. In a sense, it's like deciding what kind of a house you want to build; it makes it possible to think about the specific materials you're going to need—bricks, lumber, concrete, and so forth—and then about the design, so that in the end you get the finished product you want.

Sometimes the decision of what category of product to write is made for you. For instance, you might be enrolled in a course on American history when your instructor says: "Read up on the Civil War and prepare a paper on the war's two chief causes." Obviously, you will be writing a history report. If your favorite uncle has just sent you a birthday present and your mother hands you a pen and a piece of paper and tells you to sit down to express your appreciation, it's obvious that the item you will be writing is a thank-you note. Or, if you are an engineer with a California-based construction company whose boss asks you to fly to Chicago to see how the new shopping center is coming along, it is clear that what's wanted is a progress report.

But sometimes you will need to think through and make this first decision yourself. What if you buy a new television set, find it doesn't work properly, get no help from the store where you made the purchase, and decide to turn to the manufacturer for satisfaction? It only takes a minute's thought to realize that what you need to write is a letter of complaint. Sometimes it takes a little more think-

ing. Let's say you work at a small college, as executive
assistant to the president. One day your boss calls you in
and says that while watching the news on television the
previous evening he saw an interesting feature about the
ongoing revolution in telecommunications and how it will
change the way research is conducted. He assigns you to
look into this issue and to report back, in writing. When
you've had a chance to get back to your own office and think
for a moment, you realize that what you will need to write
is a trend report.

    As you can see, deciding what to write is not especially
hard to do. It requires merely that you think ahead a little
bit to consider the objective of whatever it is you will write.
Is your objective to report, to inform, to suggest, to persuade, to stimulate action of one kind or another? What
kind of writing product will best achieve this objective?
You will be surprised at how easy it is to answer this last
question, because in each case there is really only one
category that will fit the bill. Determine your objective—
that is, figure out the point of the exercise itself—and the
correct category of writing product will fairly leap out at
you.

    Once you know just what sort of product you are going
to write—either because someone has told you or because
you made the decision yourself based on your judgment of
what's needed—you are ready to take the second step:
picking the points that will serve as the building blocks for
your project.

STEP TWO—Picking Your Points:

    Information is what makes a piece of writing go. After
all, the purpose of writing something is to convey information. So it follows that information is the basic component
of whatever you write. Indeed, information is to any piece
of writing what cells are to a living creature, or what bricks

and lumber are to a building. It is what gives a piece of writing its shape, its thrust, its very character. Any piece of writing that includes all the necessary information in a sensible, comprehensible form will succeed, no matter what may be its other drawbacks or faults. Likewise, any piece of writing will fail that does not include the necessary information, no matter how eloquent its style and attractive its packaging. Always remember that when all is said and done, whatever you write will rise or fall on whether or not you have conveyed the information your reader needs.

In writing, information is divided into two parts: the point and the detail. A point is a piece of information that needs to be provided to a reader. A detail is the actual substance of that point. For example, in a book review you obviously need to tell your reader who wrote the book that you are reviewing. So that is a point you need to convey. The author's actual name is the detail. Or if you're writing a newspaper ad to sell your car, one point you will need to provide is the mileage; the actual number is the detail. Consider that letter of complaint to the manufacturer of the television set that you recently bought and are unhappy with. Point: why you are unhappy. Detail: the remote control gadget doesn't work.

In Step Two, your objective is merely to make a list of the points of information you are going to need for your piece of writing. Don't worry about collecting the details for these points; that's what you will do in Step Three. For the moment, you need concentrate only on picking the points you are going to need.

The key to making a list of these necessary points lies in the category of product that you are writing. That is because each category has its own information require-ments—its own list of points that must be included no matter what additional information you also may include. To illustrate this we have selected the category of "meeting report," which is something nearly everyone needs to write at one time or another. This example includes all the key points for this category, which we will outline afterward:

Report to: the Chairman
From: Vice President for Planning
Subject: Meeting of the Strategic Planning Committee

At this morning's meeting of the strategic planning committee, we decided to accelerate our growth for this year. More precisely, we decided to build not only the two factories in California we had already planned to build, but also to build a factory in Singapore.

Our decision to build this additional factory is based on your suggestion of last week that we give serious thought to a Singapore factory now, in light of our unexpected need to increase production to meet new orders, combined with the Government of Singapore's attractive financial offer made to you during your visit last month to that island country. We estimate that the new factory will cost $3 million, and that construction could begin as early as April. If so, we believe production at this plant could begin no later than January of the following year.

At our meeting, we decided to seek bids from several construction firms, and to check with our company's major bankers to learn what sort of financial package they might offer us. We expect preliminary responses from both the construction firms and the banks sometime next month.

Our decision to accelerate growth was not unanimous. Of our committee's five members — the vice presidents for planning, production, marketing, finance, and research — only three of us were originally in favor of the acceleration — planning, production, and marketing. The vice president for finance argued that construction of a factory in Singapore, now, would be too expensive; he felt the cost would diminish next year as the inflation rate falls. The vice president for research agreed with this, and added that in his judgment new production machinery would be available two years from now that would enable us to manufacture the same products at a lower cost; hence his conclusion that we would be wise to sit tight for the present.

After some discussion, the vice president for research withdrew his objection to the Singapore plant. Those of us who favored the project convinced him that the market for our product is so huge — now — that it would be a mistake to wait for two years for more efficient equipment; by that time one of our competitors would have taken our customers.

The vice president for finance continues to oppose the project.

We plan to meet again next month here at headquarters to review the situation and to assess our position.

Now, here's a breakdown of this report that lists its points. You can see how each one is absolutely necessary. (Although for the moment you need focus only on the points, for clarity's sake we have included the details, which are in italics):

1. The intended recipient *(the Chairman).*

2. The author *(Vice President for Planning).*

3. The subject *(Meeting of the Strategic Planning Committee).*

4. The key decision reached *("to accelerate our growth for this year by building a factory in Singapore").*

5. The basis for this decision *("your suggestion of last week ... in light of our unexpected need to increase production ... combined with the Government of Singapore's attractive offer ...")*

6. Relevant information about the decision:
   - an estimate of the factory's cost *("$3 million")*
   - an estimate of when construction could begin *("as early as April").*
   - an estimate of when production might start *("no later than January of the following year").*
   - the next steps to be taken *("we decided to seek bids from several construction firms, and to check with our company's major bankers ...")*
   - the likely timetable *("We expect preliminary responses ... sometime next month").*
   - a report of differing opinions among those attending the meeting *("Our decision to accelerate our growth was not unanimous ...").*
   - a report of how these differing opinions were resolved *("The vice president for research withdrew his objection. ...The vice president for finance continues to oppose the project").*

7. A sense of what to expect next *("We plan to meet again next month ... to review the situation and assess our position").*

In retrospect, it seems obvious that these points needed to be included—not merely in this report about this meeting, but in any report of any meeting. After all, the purpose of writing such a report is to let a reader know what went on, and only by providing these points can that be done. Could additional points have been provided? Of course. There is no limit to the number of points that could be provided, at least in theory. But the points that this report provides are the absolute minimum necessary to let a reader know what happened at a meeting which that reader did not attend. Obviously, no two meetings are the same. So of course the actual details will vary to reflect the unique substance and tone of each meeting. But the required points will always be the same in any report of any meeting.

To begin picking your points, first get your hands on a few examples of writing in the category you are working in. This is never hard to do, and it is always worth the effort. If you are writing a book review, collect a few reviews that others have written—it doesn't matter what book—and read them through. If you're placing an ad in a newspaper to sell your car, browse through a few newspapers to get a feel for what used-car ads look like and read like. You will be surprised at how easily you will be able to separate good examples from bad examples; how quickly you will reject examples that don't include points you know should be there, how easily you will be drawn toward examples precisely because they include the points that you—as a reader—feel a need to know.

Now, go into whatever word processing program you like and start writing out the specific points you're going to need to produce your own piece of writing. Take your time; it's better to draw up a list that is too long rather than one that's too short because you left out some crucial points. And don't hesitate to include points whose details you don't as yet know; you can always get the details you need later, and indeed that's just what you will do. For now, just be sure that the list you make includes all the points you believe your reader or readers will need or want to know.

Quite a few professional writers use an imaginary question-and-answer technique to help zero in on the points their readers will need or want to know. It is a technique that at first will seem awkward and artificial, but one that after a while will become almost second nature. Here's the way to do it: Just for a moment, forget about the idea of writing anything at all. Imagine that you are sitting with the person who is the intended reader of whatever you are going to write. The two of you are having a conversation—not about just anything, but about the subject you are going to write about. Your imaginary reader asks questions; you answer them. Sometimes you know the answers; sometimes you don't. And as you run through this conversation in your mind, all the points that you will need to produce your piece of writing will start to emerge.

To illustrate this technique, let's return to that trend report we cooked up a few pages back; where the college president asks you, his executive assistant, to look into the telecommunications revolution and its impact on research. The imaginary conversation would go something like this:

"I hope you're not too upset that I asked you to write this trend report."

"The truth is, I've never actually done one before, and I'm not quite certain how to begin."

"Look at it from my point of view. The first thing I need to know is—what exactly is going on out there."

"That's easy. It's just as you said when we talked in your office. A telecommunications revolution is under way, which means that people are using their computers in new ways to access information through telephone lines."

"Well, fine. Now you've defined the trend, and that's quite helpful to me. But when I learn that there is a new trend taking place, I can't help but wonder why it's taking place. There's always a reason."

"I know that, too. It's happening because today's technologies make it possible to combine computers and communications in new ways. And this brings down the cost of accessing information electronically."

"Excellent. But you see, each time you come forward with an interesting point it raises yet another question. Now I'm wondering how this trend is happening."

"How it's happening?"

"Of course. What I mean is, I need some details about just what it is that people can do today that was impossible

*yesterday. In other words, I need to really see how things
are being done now, as part of this trend."*

"But I don't know that."

*"I don't expect you to know it. But I do expect you to
find out and include your answer. That's not unreasonable,
is it?"*

"I suppose not. Would that be all you need?"

*"You are my eyes and ears on this thing. I'm looking
to you to tell me where the trend is going—what the future
holds."*

"I'm embarrassed to say this, but again I don't know."

*"And again, I say that I don't expect you to know. I
expect you to find out and to tell me."*

*"Okay. I'll get going on these points. But is there
anything else you're looking for in this trend report?"*

*"Yes. Just one more thing. I'd like your own personal
judgment about the trend. What do you think about it? Is
it a good trend? A bad one? Is it important? Do you see
what I'm driving at?"*

*"Yes. I think so. You want to know what the trend is,
why it's happening, how it's happening, where it's going,
and what I think of it all. These are the points you need me
to cover. Have I got it all now?"*

"Oh, yes. Indeed you do."

Relax. Enjoy yourself. If you don't like the way you
handled yourself during the imaginary conversation—do it
again. And this time go a bit more slowly. Think through
your answers; experiment with them a bit. Don't be
embarrassed; this is all happening in your mind, and no one
except you will ever know about it. Haven't you ever
wished for a second chance to say all the clever and witty
things you didn't say when you should have? Well, now's
your chance. After all, you get to make up the questions as
well as the answers, so do it your way. Play around with
your words and your ideas until you begin to feel you've got
a grip on things.

And never, never lose sight of what you started out to do. Namely, to make a list of those points you will absolutely, positively need to satisfy the requirements of the particular category into which your piece of writing falls; the points that you, as a reader, would need or want to know if someone else were writing this piece for you.

Since this step requires more thinking than actual writing, there is no need to remain glued to your chair. Quite a few professional writers spend a hefty chunk of their time walking round, jogging, grocery shopping, washing their cars, or whatever. As long as you are not actually putting words on your computer screen, you can do anything you want so long as you are able to think at the same time. Indeed, sometimes it helps a lot to get away from the table or desk. No one who reads your finished product will have the slightest idea how you spent your time during its production. No one will care, either. Keep in mind that "writing" is a step-by-step process, in which quite a few of the steps require no actual writing at all.

In any case, however you choose to do it you must eventually turn out a list of the various points you are going to need. The list should be simple, direct, and brief enough to fit easily on one screen. Once again using our trend report as an example, a list of points would look like this:

Trend Report

1. What the trend is

2. Why the trend is taking place

3. How the trend is happening

4. Where the trend is going

5. What I (the writer) think of it all

Read through the list once or twice. Make certain that you are comfortable with it. If not, go ahead and revise the list. Focus only on picking the points you're going to need for whatever category of writing you have chosen. Don't spend your time or energy worrying about anything except picking the right points.

And when you've made a list of the key points that your piece of writing must include—stop. Now you are ready for the next step, which is to go out and collect the details you haven't got yet.

STEP THREE—*Collecting Your Details:*

The single greatest cause of panic-stricken paralysis among writers is neither lack of confidence nor lack of inspiration. Rather, it is lack of a specific detail the writer needs at a particular moment to flesh out a point he or she knows must be made, combined with a stubborn refusal to face up to the problem and to treat it with the only remedy that works: namely, going out and collecting that detail.

To grasp the importance of this go-out-and-get-what-you-need business, imagine for a moment that you are in your kitchen, preparing a dinner party for some friends. Now, a dinner party is a category of meal, and just like a category of writing it has its own requirements: something to start, a main course, a dessert. Let's say your menu will be soup, followed by roast beef with potatoes and carrots, then vanilla ice cream with chocolate sauce for dessert. It's 5 p.m. and your guests are due to arrive at eight o'clock. You suddenly realize that, although you've been grocery shopping twice for this dinner party, you have somehow forgotten to buy the roast. Alas, there are no plausible substitutes in the freezer—no lamb chops, no steaks, no hamburger. Clearly, you have two ways to go: make do without the roast, or scramble out to the supermarket. You really haven't got much choice, have you? Unless you want to take a chance that your guests are total idiots and won't notice that the main course is missing. Obviously, you decide to dash out to the supermarket despite the late hour and the inconvenience.

Now imagine that the item you forgot to buy during your shopping expeditions is the chocolate sauce. Since vanilla ice cream tastes delicious all by itself (and since no one will ever know you'd planned to serve chocolate sauce, unless you tell them), you say to heck with it. You didn't want the extra calories, anyway.

What ingredients are to a meal, details are to a piece of writing. Some are more important than others. Some are expendable if the effort required to get them is too great. Others require the effort at whatever cost. Moreover, some of the crucial ones aren't obviously crucial as is, say, a main-course roast to a dinner party. What if you hadn't bothered to buy salt? Or sugar and cream for the coffee? It can be such a small ingredient—or detail—that makes the difference between smooth sailing and rough going, between success and failure.

Collecting details for a piece of writing is very much like grocery shopping for a dinner party. You start by making a list of the requirements for the category you have chosen—which is what you did in Step Two. Then you check off those items for which the details (the ingredients, as it were) are already on hand. Then, finally, you go out to get whatever you need but haven't yet got. If in the end you discover that you forgot a detail—like forgetting an ingredient when you're shopping, it happens to everyone now and then—you then must decide whether it's crucial or merely desirable. If it's crucial, you scramble out to get it whatever the cost or inconvenience. If it's merely desirable, you use your best judgment.

These are the key principles of collecting details for any piece of writing:

- Anticipate
- Be Energetic

- Be Dogged
- Be Imaginative

Anticipate: Keep in mind that the writing process begins when the need arises to write something; not when you finally sit down to turn out a first draft. The sooner you begin to collect the details you're going to need, the better off you will be; the less time and effort you will need to devote to collection and, therefore, the more time and effort you can pour into later phases of the writing process.

By anticipating the details you're going to need, you give yourself a head start on collecting them. Let's say you show up one evening at your child's school for a meeting of the parent-teacher association. The PTA president takes you aside, tells you that the parent who usually writes up the meeting-report for the PTA bulletin has called in sick, and asks you to write the report and have it ready for printing and distribution the next day. Now, it's likely that the meeting will last for roughly one hour, and that you will be working late into the night to complete your report. It's also likely that the participants in the meeting will be hard to find after the meeting ends—or, worse, fast asleep. By anticipating what details you're going to need, you can collect them before the meeting breaks up. For example, you are obviously going to need the names and school-or-PTA titles of key participants. No big deal; just be sure to ask someone—and to write down his or her answers—either just before the meeting starts or just after it ends. If during the course of the meeting somebody mentions "the Bradley project"—which you have never heard of before—make sure to grab that person before he or she escapes to get a brief explanation.

Never be embarrassed to tell people what you are doing and to ask them for help. How do you actually do this? You do it the easy way; you just go up to them and ask: "Excuse me, my name is So-and-So and I've been asked to write up a report on this meeting. Would you be kind enough to tell me the correct spelling of your name and your precise title? Thanks so much." Don't worry; it almost always works. Most people are very nice and very pleasant. Or, if someone says something you don't grasp, get hold of that individual after the meeting, tell him or her your problem, and ask for some help. You'll get it. And don't be embarrassed to admit that you're still not sure you understand; just explain that you will be writing your report during the evening, and ask for a telephone number where the person can be reached. You'll get the number — and with gratitude to boot. Intelligent people would rather you reported what they said accurately, even if it causes some minor inconvenience.

Your ability to anticipate the details you're going to need, and thus your ability to efficiently collect them as you move along, will grow dramatically as you become familiar and comfortable with the writing process. You will be surprised by how easy it becomes to spot necessary details as, so to speak, you roll your grocery cart down the aisle. And when you sit down to actually to write out that list of points you're going to need, you will find that you already have in hand more and more of the details, too.

Be Energetic: Keep in mind that there is a lot more to "writing" than tapping away on your computer keyboard. You must devote much of your effort to collecting the information you will need to choose your words and write your sentences. And this is more of a physical than a mental chore. So don't be lazy. If there's a detail you know you are going to need—go get it. For instance, if you are writing a review of a new restaurant your readers will need to know if the place accepts telephone reservations. There is just one way to find out, and that's by asking the owner or manager. So ask. In a trip-report on a visit to the Empire State Building, you must assume your reader already knows that the building is tall. So reach across to your almanac or encyclopedia—or trot off to the nearest library—and look it up.

Or if you are a real estate agent writing a sales brochure for a farm that's just come on to the market, don't settle for saying that the place has "several hundred" acres. Your readers will want to know precisely how many acres there are. What's that? You say you forgot to ask the owner when you toured the place? Big deal; we all goof up from time to time. Go back and ask him, or simply call him up. And if by some odd chance he doesn't know the answer to your question, hire a surveyor to measure the place. Or, if you are trying to convince your boss to rent office space in one building or another, keep in mind that he will need to know precisely how the rents compare with each other. Get the numbers and put them in your memo. (And if driving time from the office to the airport is important, get in your car and make the comparison yourself; there's nothing like first-hand research to give your report credibility and weight.)

Get out of your chair. Use a telephone, use your feet, jump in your car or saddle up your horse. Look it up, check it out, pin it down. You will more than make up for the lost time when you finally sit down to write your first draft. The biggest time-waster of all is sitting down and becoming paralyzed because you didn't spend the energy to gather up details you knew darn well you were going to need.

Be Dogged: Collecting details can be fun. Indeed, for some writers this is far and away the most enjoyable phase of the entire process. But collecting details can also be a ferocious pain in the neck. You slug your way through rush-hour traffic to the library—and discover when you get inside that the volume of the encyclopedia you need is missing. Or that some thoughtless idiot has ripped out the page of the almanac that would have would have given you the precise height and number of stories of the Empire State Building. Or you telephone the individual who has the detail you need, only to be told that the blinking so-and-so has just left the country to go hiking in the Himalayas and won't be back for six weeks at least. No, you are told by coolly efficient (and utterly useless) secretary, there is no one else in the office who can help you.

Don't be discouraged. And for heaven's sake, don't give up too easily. Very often the difference between a successful piece of writing and a failure is not the literary quality of the prose or even the skill of its organization, but rather the doggedness of its research. When you come down to it, there are really very few details that can't be found; mostly it's a question of time and effort.

The decision of how hard to work for a needed detail —how much time and effort to devote—is always a matter of judgment. Human nature being what it is—more precisely, most of us being more or less on the lazy side—the tendency is always to give up when the going gets rough. Good writers learn to be just a bit more dogged. When they can't get a necessary detail the easy way, they do it the hard way. This means a bit more time and effort, such as going to another library, or looking in two or three reference books, or making a few more telephone calls, or whatever. You will be amazed by how often just a little bit of extra time and effort pays off in the end.

Keep in mind that when you write for someone—no matter what you write; no matter who you write it for—you become your reader's eyes, ears, legs, and even intellect. In a very real sense, you are acting as an extension of your reader. So do the kind of job you would want someone else to do for you.

Be Imaginative: Few things do more for a piece of writing than newly discovered details, or well known details described in wholly new and interesting ways. If you are writing a letter to a business executive trying to convince him to locate his new factory in your town, think how persuasive it would be if you could write that six of his ten largest customers were headquartered within a radius of 50 miles, or that each year the local college graduates roughly 100 students with precisely the skills his work force would require. Or if you are working with a church group that's trying to raise money to help feed hungry children in Africa, and you've been asked to write a letter soliciting donations from members of the congregation, rather than just ask for money notice how much more effective it is to point out that $5 will keep a child alive for nearly two weeks, and that $20 will keep an entire family from starving for that period. These are the sorts of details that carry weight; that make a difference to the reader. It is your job as a writer to go beyond the obvious details, and to think up new ones that will enlighten your reader and take him or her in the direction you want to go.

Discovering new details often is just a matter of asking questions. You casually ask the owner of the house for whom you are writing a sales brochure whether he is the original owner—and discover that he bought the place from a famous actor. Now that's worth mentioning in the sales brochure. Or when you ask the owner of the restaurant you're reviewing how he happened to open the place, he matter-of-factly tells you he used to be chief chef at the White House, but decided to leave Washington because the climate there was bad for his daughter's allergies. Wow! Obviously, you don't get lucky every time. But you'd be surprised how often you come up with something interesting—and therefore useful —when you actively look for it; when you open your eyes and your energies to whatever may be available.

Always keep an eye open for imaginative ways to present details that are already well known. If you are trying to describe how many bars of chocolate a candy manufacturer has sold, don't just give the number; give your reader a visual idea of how many bars that really is: "The company has sold 55 million chocolate bars—enough bars to fill up Yankee Stadium from home plate to the top of the bleachers." Or, if for a research paper on the Common Market's economic problems you were trying to describe the amount of surplus butter in Western Europe—what economists call the "butter mountain"—why not point out that this "mountain" is so huge that if spread over Vienna it would cover the entire city to a depth of six inches. All you need to come up with imaginative ways to present your details is the idea itself; a pocket calculator helps.

Don't be afraid to try something different. Reach for a new detail, or a new way to describe a well-known detail. You will enlighten your reader and, more importantly, hold your reader's interest. And by doing so you will guide your reader in the direction you have chosen to go.

To illustrate these principles of collecting details, let us return again to that trend report whose points we picked back in Step Two. And let's put ourselves in the writer's position. The trick will be to take each point in turn, and to pour on whatever effort is required to get the necessary information. Our objective is a list made up of the points and, below each point, its particular details. Remember, this list will be for our own use—no one else will ever see it. So we don't need to worry about format, neatness, or style. We just need to make certain that the list meets our need for information.

To refresh your memory, we decided that the points of a trend report are:

1. What the trend is;
2. Why the trend is taking place;
3. How the trend is happening;
4. Where the trend is going;
5. What I (the writer) think of it all.

In this particular example, we've got a leg up because we already know the details for the first point; we know what the trend is: A telecommunications revolution is under way, meaning that people are using their computers in new ways to access information through telephone lines. Indeed, it was the report about this trend that the college president saw on television that triggered the need to write. Since we already have this ingredient on hand, so to speak, we can move along to the second point. To learn why the trend is taking place, we would do what the television reporter presumably did. We would talk with someone at the telephone company who is familiar with the trend and who can explain it to us in terms that we can understand. We would also ask this person to explain how the trend is happening. But in addition, it wouldn't hurt to stop by a local computer store to ask the manager for his thoughts on the subject. After all, it is to this kind of store that people who are using computers to communicate would come first, since without the machines they can't get started.

For details on where the trend is going, we could go to the library and look up "telecommunications" in the catalog, browse through some magazines that might have articles on the subject, and ask the librarian for any material that might be available. (We might even find that the librarian, being an up-to-date professional, is herself using a computer to access information electronically. If so, she would be a good source of information and insight.) For the last point—our own evaluation of the trend—we would rely again on all these sources, and perhaps also on the judgments of some "experts" we have managed to locate, for example in the computer sciences department of the college. We would distill their thinking into our own personal point of view.

We end up with a list that looks like this:

1. WHAT THE TREND IS

A telecommunications revolution is underway ... meaning that people are using their computers in new ways to access information through telephone lines.

2. WHY THE TREND IS TAKING PLACE

The trend is happening because new technologies enable computers and telephones to work together.... This means that telephone lines are used to convey data, rather than spoken words. ... This has led to establishment of electronic libraries, data bases, bulletin board systems and other such information resources ... computers themselves now can access and store electronic information quickly and efficiently.

3. HOW THE TREND IS HAPPENING

Companies are springing up all over the country that provide information electronically. Some are electronic versions of libraries from which books, articles and even software products can be read and "downloaded" by customers who pay hourly on-line fees ... also emergence of so-called bulletin board systems—BBSs—which enable people with a common interest to communicate with one another and to share ideas and information. Meanwhile, telephone companies are upgrading their lines to carry the increasing flow of data ... and computer manufacturers developing cheaper and faster modems to enable users to communicate more easily and more efficiently.

4. WHERE THE TREND IS GOING

Trend is moving very swiftly now ... in just a few years nearly all printed information will be available electronically—newspapers, magazines, textbooks, research papers.... which means students doing research will be able to conduct much of their research working at their desks through their computers ... more extensive research than ever before, since they will be able to access more information sources.

5. WHAT I (THE WRITER) THINK OF IT ALL

Remarkable trend that will enable students to do better research . . . enable them to access not only the university library but libraries all over the world—and without leaving their desks, using just a computer connected to a telephone line. Important that we train students to use computers in this fashion. . . . University may need more courses in this subject . . . will take some getting used to, but overall a genuine revolution that we ought to celebrate and support.

When we have made our list, we'll read through it once or twice. We'll do it carefully, taking a few extra minutes not only to read but to think. We might even get up to take a walk or get a drink of water. Our focus at this point is on substance rather than style. We just need to be certain that the details we've collected explain the points that we've picked. Again, we won't worry about format, neatness or style. This list is for our own use, and no one but us will ever see it. If we can see some way to improve or expand what we've written, we'll go ahead and make the change. If it looks all right, we'll leave it alone.

Don't be surprised—or discouraged—if all this thinking, choosing, collection, and list-making activity that we've outlined in Part One of *How to Write* seems a bit awkward or difficult at first. As we said at the outset, organizing-for-the-job is far and away the most "invisible" part of the writing process. Moreover, for reasons we cannot understand it's the part that schools and universities rarely if ever teach. Little wonder, then, that so many people have trouble writing; they are not taught the first part of the process and are somehow expected to start with second part and go on from there—which simply can't be done.

If it takes you a while to decide what it is you are going to write, to make a list of necessary points, and then to gather up your details—don't worry about it. The time you spend learning to master these steps and techniques will serve you well. Just remember the Meyers' first (and only) law of writing: any piece of writing that conveys the necessary information in some reasonable and coherent order will succeed no matter what its other flaws and drawbacks.

And when at last you have decided what it is you're going to write, made your list of necessary points for this particular category of writing, and collected all your details, you have completed the vital, "invisible" part of the writing process that all professionals know makes the difference between failure and success. Indeed, after completing this part of the process you have actually got in hand everything you need to begin turning out your first draft. In Part Two we will show you how to put it all together.

PART TWO

Turning out a
First Draft

Turning out a first draft is far and away the most decisive part of the writing process. For this is when you begin to commit yourself to a specific course of action; to a detailed and precise architecture of the finished product.

To be sure, you can write second drafts, third drafts, fourth drafts—even tenth drafts if you want to. And, once you are familiar with the skills and techniques of draft-polishing, you will have little difficulty making each successive draft better than the one before. But no matter how many drafts you write, it is the first draft that always has the biggest influence on your finished product. The others are merely modifications and improvements of the original, first-draft architecture. In this sense, turning out a first draft is a bit like constructing a building; once you've put up the walls and laid down the roof, whatever changes you make are at best important modifications. You can improve the building—often dramatically and with surprisingly little effort—but not change its architecture in any fundamental way. You can make a telephone booth a better telephone booth, a hamburger stand a better hamburger stand, and a factory a better factory. But you cannot really turn a telephone booth into a hamburger stand, or a hamburger stand into a factory, or a factory into a telephone booth.

In other words, shortcomings and mistakes in the *execution* of a first draft can be overcome and repaired; that is precisely what second, third, fourth, even tenth drafts are for. But if you make an *architectural* mistake in the first draft—that is, if you build the wrong thing, however well you build it—you are more or less stuck. Why can't you just tear up the entire mess and start over again? In theory, you can. You may even be able to do it in practice. But as a general rule, by the time you've written out a first draft you have expended too much time and intellectual energy to throw out what you've done and start all over again from scratch. At this point, you will be scrambling to make the best of what you've got, either because you have run short of time or because you have burned up too much intellectual energy. Again, you can improve a first draft, often dramatically and with surprisingly little effort. So flaws and shortcomings in the execution are nothing at all to worry about. At this point, you need be concerned only with choosing the right architecture. That is your primary objective in turning out a first draft.

As you will see in the steps that follow, turning out a first draft is primarily a focusing, sketching-out and construction process, during which you will need to:

> *1. Figure out your theme,*
> *2. Make your outline,*
> *3. Write your draft.*

STEP ONE—Figuring Out Your Theme:

Every piece of writing has a theme. It's always in there somewhere. The difference between successful pieces of writing and unsuccessful pieces is this: in successful ones the theme is written out so clearly that the reader has no trouble grasping it, while in unsuccessful pieces of writing the theme is so obscure, so buried and scattered throughout the text, that either it can't be grasped at all by the reader or the effort required to grasp it is more than any reader can be expected to make. It is the difference between showing someone a building—or showing someone a pile of wood, bricks, nails and mortar and asking him or her to imagine how the building would look if only you had taken the trouble to put it all together.

Think of it this way: since the point of any piece of writing is to communicate ideas and information, to succeed you must do the reader's work—that is to say, his thinking—for him. You must show him what you mean, not throw a bunch of words, sentences, and paragraphs at him and hope the poor devil will have the time, skill and inclination to figure it out for himself. That is why the first step in turning out a first draft is for you to figure out your own theme so you can put it right up front, literally at the very top of your piece of writing In this way—and only in this way—can you be sure that your reader will see clearly what you mean.

A theme captures in just a few words or sentences—in other words, a theme summarizes—what it is you want to say about the subject at hand. Thus it is not the same thing as the subject itself. It is more like the explanation of the subject; it answers the question, "Well, what about it?" Let's say you get a telephone call from a friend who is president of the local Professional Women's Association. She tells you that the group holds a luncheon every other Wednesday, and she invites you to be their guest at the next session and to deliver a short talk on the subject of "Working Mothers." You accept the invitation (you hate speaking in public, but you owe her a favor so you can't say no) and now you sit down to write your speech. Here are a few of the possible themes a speech on the subject of "Working Mothers" might have:

Working mothers have gone from a small if interesting phenomenon to a major segment of today's work force. In doing so, this has fundamentally changed not only our country's work force, but our family lifestyles. As more and more mothers take jobs—and as more and more women continue working after starting families—these changes will become more profound and more lasting.

• With this as your theme, you would go on to provide the statistical evidence to show just how rapidly the number of working mothers has grown. You would explain how family lifestyles have changed now that so many mothers are holding jobs, and you would probably project what future changes are likely as still more mothers join the work force. No doubt you would offer your own opinion of these developments. In effect what you are writing here, for oral delivery as a speech, is a trend report.

Now that the majority of mothers work, the time has come for a program of action to bring business practices and regulations into line with reality. At present our system, designed for an age when women with children stayed at home, fails utterly to take the needs of working mothers into account. This is both unfair and counter-productive.

• With this as your theme, you would go on to outline why and how the present system is unfair to working mothers. Then you would outline a series of reforms designed to modernize business practices and regulations, for example a program to provide flexible working hours for women with children, more liberal maternity-leave benefits, and expanded tax deductions for day-care expenditures. You would explain how these changes would be more fair, and how they would enable working mothers, and thus our country's economy, to become more productive. In effect what you are writing here, again for oral delivery as a speech, is a course-of-action memo.

I'm sick and tired of hearing working mothers complain about their problems. Ironically, the complaining doesn't come from all those women who work because their families need the money they earn to eat. The complaining comes from those affluent, upwardly-mobile women who work not because they must, but because they want to; because staying at home with their children doesn't offer enough satisfaction for them. Of course these women have every right to work, but that doesn't mean society must change to accommodate their efforts to have their cake and eat it, too. Mothers who choose to stay at home with young children also "work" —hard—and it's time we devoted a bit more attention to their problems and needs.

• With this as your theme, you would go on to sharply criticize working mothers who are part of the current movement to change business practices and regulations to accommodate their own unique needs. You would explain why you don't share their view, and why you believe acceptance of their program would be detrimental. You would offer a strong defense of mothers who choose to stay at home with their children, and you might go on to highlight some of their unique needs and perhaps offer some suggestions for how to ease their burdens. In effect what you would be writing here, for oral delivery as a speech, is a personal-point-of-view paper. (And given the forum for which this paper/speech is intended, you might also be writing your obituary. But that's another matter.)

As you can see, knowing what the subject is tells you very little about the theme. Why? Because you can write your piece to make it go in virtually any direction. But the one thing that you cannot do is to expect your reader to figure out, by him or her self, the direction in which you have chosen to go. You—the writer— have to do this for your reader by clearly articulating your own theme. Here's another set of theme examples, this time of newspaper editorial-page articles on the complex and always contro-versial subject of "International Trade":

Trade is important to our country because it helps create jobs. Yet our political leaders pay too little attention to securing those global trading agreements that would enable us to manufacture and export more of our country's products. Our leaders must get to work negotiating the best possible agreements, and soon.

• An editorial with this as its theme would focus on explaining why trade is so important. It would go on to describe just what it is the political leaders aren't doing—

or aren't doing properly. And it would outline the kinds of trade agreements that ought to be negotiated. The editorial might include a projection of what the consequences would be of failing to secure such agreements.

On the other hand, with the very same subject—International Trade—the theme could be this:

The only way to increase our exports will be to produce the best quality products. And the key to top-quality manufacturing is an educated, highly trained work force. Thus we need to increase our spending on education and technical training to create the kind of work force that will be capable of turning out the export products that can compete in the global marketplace.

• An editorial with this as its theme would focus on the role of top-quality products in the global marketplace. Then it would go on to articulate the case for expanded education programs, and explain how such programs actually would improve the quality and value of the nation's work force. The editorial might conclude by listing the specific kinds of education and training programs most likely to produce the best results.

Or even this could be the theme of an editorial on International Trade:

Our chief economic problem is the flood of products that arrive here from other countries. These imported products are costing jobs among our own workers, and are helping to put many of our country's manufacturers out of business. If we are to protect our economy from foreign competition, the government should become more aggressive in stopping these imports.

• An editorial with this as its theme would go on to articulate the case for protectionism—for government measures such as tariffs and other import barriers to slow down or stop the flood of products from other countries. The editorial might list some of the companies or industries that have been hurt by foreign products, and it might project the extent of damage in future years should the level of imports be allowed to increase.

It is obvious that figuring out your theme is an especially critical step. The good news is that it isn't very hard to do. You just have to be very careful. Keep in mind that your goal is to come up with a few short sentences that capture, clearly and precisely, whatever it is you mean. The best way to start is with the list of points that you picked back in Part One. Look at your subject—which of course is the very first point on your list—and then ask yourself the key question: "Well, what about this subject? What's my objective?" Are you trying to talk your reader into something? Or out of something? Are you trying to persuade, to be helpful, merely to convey information, to trigger some specific course of action, or to expound your own personal point of view?

If the theme doesn't leap out at you—and it rarely does—then read through the various details that you collected to see if they provide a clue. They often do. And if the theme still hasn't leapt out at you, try doing what you did in Part One, when you organized for the job. That is, settle down, relax, and have yourself an imaginary conversation with whomever is the intended reader of whatever it is you are planning to write. Here's the imaginary conversation that we had with you, just before we sat down to write the first draft of this very book you're reading now:

"So tell me, what sort of a piece are you writing?"

"It's a book. More precisely, it's a how-to book designed to show people how to write."

"How very interesting. Tell me, what's your theme?"

"Well, er, you see, what we're trying to do is, um, to —"

"Don't panic. We'll work it out. Tell me, have you got some unique approach to the subject?"

"Sure we do. You see, everybody thinks that writing is some sort of mysterious art; a sort of talent that either you have or you don't."

"But that's true, isn't it?"

"No. It isn't true at all. Writing is just a process—like cooking, or carpentry, or cleaning a house. Of course, not everyone can be a great cook, or a great carpenter, or a great house-cleaner. But anybody can learn the process, and with a bit of practice do a fairly decent job."

"I see. So this is your approach?"

"Yes, I suppose it is."

"But what exactly is this process, as you call it? Can you articulate it for me?"

"This isn't the time to go into too much detail. But in general it works like this: First, you organize for the job. Then you turn out a first draft. Then you polish that draft until you've got a decent, effective finished product. As we say, you do all this through a series of little steps taken in the proper sequence."

"It sounds like we're beginning to focus on a theme. If I understand you correctly, it runs like this: Writing well requires neither art nor talent. That's because writing is a process like any other. Thus it can be learned. In essence, there are three parts to the writing process, with each part containing a number of specific steps. The three parts are organizing for the job, turning out a first draft, and polishing the draft into an effective finished product."

"Hey, it sounds like we've figured out our theme."

"I believe we have."

Don't be surprised if it takes a fair amount of time and effort to figure out your theme. Don't be discouraged, either. And above all, don't give up. In the history of writing, there has never been a piece of writing that didn't have a theme that could be articulated in a few, clearly written sentences. And there never will be such a piece. It's just that some themes are a bit harder than others to work out.

So take your time. Remember, there is no rule which requires you to stare at your computer watching the cursor blink away in the upper left-hand corner of a blank screen, while you think things out. Do whatever is most comfortable for you. if you need to sit down and type words onto your computer screen—go right ahead. But don't be reluctant to get up and walk around, or jog, or wash the dishes, or whatever. As we said earlier, quite a few professional writers find that physical activity of one sort or another helps them to think clearly—and this is one step in the writing process where clear thinking is essential.

Now let's return yet another time to that trend report we launched back in Part One. Having chosen our category, picked our points, and collected our details, we need to figure out our theme. Since it isn't leaping out at us—no big deal; as we said, themes rarely do—it's time for another imaginary conversation with our intended reader.

"Hello again. How's your project coming along?"

"Not so well, I'm afraid. I'm having a bit of trouble figuring out my theme."

"Well that happens. Tell me, what did you find out when you were out there collecting all your details? What did you learn?"

"I've got my list, but — "

"Then look at it. Study it. What does it tell you? Try to distill the meaning of what you found out. Stand back from it a bit. That usually helps."

"Let me think for a moment. I learned that people are using their computers in new ways to access information through telephone lines. Is that what you mean?"

"It's precisely what I mean. Just keep going."

"Okay. The trend is happening because new technologies are making it possible for computers and telephones to work together. People are setting up electronic libraries, data bases, and bulletin board systems that enable anyone with a modem-equipped computer to connect. How am I doing?"

"Beautifully. What else?"

"Just my own view of it, which is on balance the trend is a good one."

"Why is that?"

"Why?"

"Yes, why. Look, I can read anything you write, but I can't read your mind. When you make a judgment, you've got to give me, in writing, some explanation of why you hold that point of view. Now, you were saying that on balance the trend is a good one?"

"Yes, that's right. The trend will enable people -- students especially—to do much better research. They'll be able to access not only the university library but libraries and data bases around the world. And through bulletin board systems they'll be able to talk with other people directly who share interests and who might have the information the students need. Have I got it now?"

"If you think about it for a moment, you'll realize that you've figured out your theme. Just catch your breath and spell it out in one burst."

"Okay, here goes. We are in the midst of a telecommunications revolution in which people are using computers in new ways to access information through telephone lines. By doing so people can connect to libraries, data bases, bulletin board systems and other electronic sources to acquire information on virtually any subject, at a very low cost. The trend is moving swiftly, and in a few years

virtually all printed information will be available electronically. This is a good trend that will enable research to be conducted more effectively and more efficiently. Is that my theme?"

"It certainly is."

Keep in mind that writing takes a certain tenacity. Things don't always work out right the first time; you make a mistake and wind up with a bit of a mess, or realize you missed something along the way. There's nothing to do but shrug off the mistake, or clean up the mess, or go back over the part to add something you realized you missed the first time. In short, there's nothing to do but to try again. So if you don't like the way that your imaginary conversation with your intended reader works out, have a second or even a third imaginary conversation. Likewise with whatever you type out on your computer. Nobody will ever see the material you toss out or delete, so don't be embarrassed to try something even if it turns out to be a flop. Work out as many variations as you need until you get the theme that you want.

And how will you know when you've got the theme that you want? You're not going to like the answer to this one: the answer is, you can't be sure you've got the "right" theme. At least, you can't be sure just yet. You need to go on a bit, at least to the next step. For it is only as you work your way through the next step—which is making an outline—that you can determine for sure whether the theme you've just worked out is the "right" one for the piece you are writing.

STEP TWO—Making an Outline:

An outline serves two key purposes. First, an outline serves as a check—a test—on what you have done up to now. Just like the steel girders of a skyscraper, a writing outline suggests the shape and size of the product-to-be. If it looks like what you had in mind—fine. You keep going. But if the outline suggests a product-to-be that isn't what you want or need—boy, will it ever be visible to you. In other words, if you are on the right track an outline will make this clear. But if in fact you have made an important error of judgment along the way and wound up with the "wrong" theme—wrong, that is, for the piece you want to write—this is when you will catch it. And you will be able to make the necessary changes before you've strayed too far off course and burned up too much time and energy to turn back.

Second, an outline acts as a skeleton for the draft itself. For when you have gotten your outline right it serves— again, like the steel girders of a skyscraper—as a visible, sturdy frame that you can beef up and flesh out until it becomes a semi-finished and then a finished product.

To make your outline, begin by writing out a title at the top of your screen. You needn't worry about whether it's an especially wonderful title; it's for your own use, and you will have plenty of time to come up with a better title later on. For now, just put down the first title that pops into your head. (You will be surprised by how often the first title that pops into your head turns out to be the best one). Now write out your theme below the title. This will amount to a fairly solid paragraph. Then write out the points you've picked along with the details that will flesh out these points. In doing so, this time combine the points and the details, as appropriate, so that what you write appears in complete, understandable sentences. For convenience's sake, continue to number the points.

This theme-points-details list will work for you as an outline by serving as a skeleton and thus illuminating what your finished product will look like. Of course, if you don't like the way your product is going to look, this will be your chance to fix it. In many cases, you will be able to do this simply by shifting around or modifying the numbered points. But if this shifting and modifying doesn't do the trick, you may be certain that the problem lies with the theme you have developed. If so, this is when you "stop the presses" to go back and develop the theme that will be just right for your piece of writing.

Returning once again to our trend report, here is what the outline would look like.

The On-Line Research Revolution

A telecommunications revolution is under way in which people are using computers to access information through telephone lines. By doing so people can connect electronically to libraries, data bases, bulletin board systems and other such on-line sources to acquire information on virtually any subject, at a very low cost. The trend is moving swiftly, and in a few years virtually all printed information will be available electronically. This is a good trend that will enable students to conduct research more effectively and efficiently.

1. A telecommunications revolution is under way, in which people are using their computers in new ways to access information through telephone lines.

2. The trend is happening because new technologies enable computers and telephones to work together. This, in turn, has led to the establishment of electronic information sources such as libraries and data bases.

3. Companies are springing up all over the country that provide information electronically. Some of these are electronic versions of libraries from which books, articles and even software products can be read and "downloaded" by customers who pay hourly on-line fees. And the telephone companies are upgrading their lines to carry the increasing flow of data.

4. As for where the trend is going, we are heading for a time when all printed information will be available electronically, and when people with an interest in any particular subject or issue can connect electronically to other people with the same interest, no matter where in the world they may be.

5. As for my own judgment, it seems clear that students with on-line access capabilities will be able to conduct research in wholly new and exciting ways.

Now let's read through the outline once or twice. How does it look? Surely you can see what a first draft based on this outline would be like. Is this the product we have in mind to write? Will it serve our purpose? Will it make sense to our reader? Are we comfortable with it? Let's not worry about little details and small points, but is anything important missing? No? Good. Whoops—hang on a minute! Should we include a section that outlines the emerging technologies that will fuel the telecommunications revolution in coming years, for instance the wireless communications technologies that will enable electronic access even without telephone lines? We could slip in a section like this after the current Section 4. Let's think for a moment. No doubt such a section would be accurate and interesting. But is it necessary? Well, necessary is putting it a bit too strongly. So it's a judgment call. We've been prudent to consider adding in the section, but in this case let's give ourselves a break and leave it out after all.

Now, is everything in the best possible order? What's that? You'd rather we tell the reader how the trend is happening before telling him why the trend is happening? Okay; there's no law which requires the "why" to come before the "how" of a trend report. Just reverse points 2 and 3. Is that better? Fine. Now, would it read better if point 4 were moved up, so that it comes between the new points 2 and 3? Well, maybe so. Let's try it. Hmmm, not bad but it's no big improvement either. Let's leave point 4 where it is. Finally, let's stand back from the outline one more time to see if it looks like the "right" skeleton for the piece of writing we want. If it doesn't, we'll probably have to go back to re-work the theme. Happily, it looks all right. So have we got our outline? Yes, indeed. We sure do.

Now what? We go on to the next step, which is writing out the first draft.

STEP THREE—Writing Out the First Draft:

When you've finished making your outline and begin to write out your first draft, the entire nature of the writing process changes. You go, so to speak, from design to construction. For most writers, this is a key turning point. Some writers find all the remaining steps—the construction steps, if you will—easier than the design steps. Other writers find these construction steps the hardest ones to take. There is very little you can do about this. It is entirely a matter of style, personality, skill, and preference. The trick to coping is simply to understand the shift that occurs at this point in the writing process; then you can either celebrate or, alas, make the best of it.

It is never easy to write a first draft. But the whole purpose of everything we have done up to now is to make this step a manageable one to take. In essence, you write a first draft by expanding, beefing up, and fleshing out your outline. As we said earlier, this is more of a construction job than it is a design job. So it is more a matter of effort than of inspiration. For those of you who would rather "think" than "work," writing a first draft will actually be a little boring and perhaps a bit tedious. And for those of you who despise "thinking" and prefer "working", writing a first draft will come as something of a relief, or even a bit of a lark.

The best advice we've ever heard for this particular step came, oddly enough, from a long-distance runner. Asked by a weekend jogger how on earth he had the energy and stamina to run twenty miles, the long-distance runner smiled and said: "Good heavens, I couldn't possibly get going if I thought about running twenty miles. I run one mile —but I do it twenty times."

You write a first draft by expanding, beefing up, and fleshing out one section of your outline at a time. You treat each section as though it were a separate entity, and you spend as much time as necessary with each section. Some will be easy to write; others will be hard. Some will come out so well, that when you settle down later on to polish your draft, these sections will need little if any work. Other sections will come out less well, and so will need more fixing up later on. You just do the best you can with a section, and when you are comfortable with that section— or in the case of hard sections, when you feel you've "had it" for the moment—you go on to the next section.

To begin, simply copy out the title and theme just as they appear in your outline:

The On-Line Research Revolution

A telecommunications revolution is under way in which people are using computers to access information through telephone lines. By doing so people can connect electronically to libraries, data bases, bulletin board systems and other such on-line sources to acquire information on virtually any subject, at a very low cost. The trend is moving swiftly, and in a few years virtually all printed information will be available electronically. This is a good trend that will enable students to conduct research more effectively and efficiently.

Now, under your title and theme you expand, beef up, and flesh out each section of your outline. Take each section one at a time, and use each point—that is, each sentence or two that represents a section of your outline— to launch the sections of your draft. If your point is sound, you will have no trouble carrying it forward into a full paragraph or even into two or three full paragraphs. After all, these paragraphs are merely extensions, explanations, and elaborations of the outline itself. Again, for convenience's sake continue to number the sections:

1. A telecommunications revolution is under way, in which people are using their computers in new ways to access information through telephone lines. So much information is now available electronically that this constitutes a new form of media, one that is changing the very nature of research.

• What we've done here, as you can see, has been to expand somewhat on the fact of the telecommunications revolution. By doing so, we have set the stage for the next section:

2. New technologies that enable computers and telephones to work together are fueling the trend. More precisely, anyone with a modem-equipped computer can "dial up" to a wide range of electronic information sources such as libraries, data bases and bulletin board systems. These sources generally charge modest hourly fees, and in some cases extra fees for access to certain information or for the right to print out information or to "download" it onto one's own computer.

• Notice how we've changed some of the wording from our outline. That is a perfectly correct—and quite common —thing to do. We made the changes so that our piece flowed more smoothly. Our objective was to expand, beef up, and flesh out what was in our outline. We did this by explaining what the new technology is—a modem—and

by telling a bit about how these electronic sources work.
Now we roll forward to the next section:

*3. Companies are springing up all over the country
that provide information electronically. Some of these
companies offer what amount to electronic versions of
libraries from which books, articles and even software
products can be read and "downloaded." Other companies are setting up bulletin board systems, which are a form
of electronic meeting place where people with a shared
interest can exchange ideas and information. For instance,
there are bulletin boards for people interested in business,
education, cooking, music and even some television shows
such as* **Star Trek**. *The* **Star Trek** *bulletin board has
separate sections for each of the shows' characters, such as
Captain Kirk and Captain Picard, and even one section to
focus on the efforts of Mr. Data to become human.*

*At the same time, telephone companies are upgrading
their lines to carry the increasing flow of data. They are
even preparing for a time when video can be transmitted
over these lines onto computers. And the computer makers
are starting to get their act together by developing the
technologies that will enable computers to function like
televisions.*

• We're rolling now, and as you can see we did quite
a bit of beefing up and fleshing out. We told our reader quite
a bit more about just what is happening out there; just what
it is that the electronic sources, the telephone companies,
and the computer makers are doing to carry the trend
forward. We even launched a second paragraph. After all,
there is no reason to limit each section of our outline to just
one paragraph; sometimes it will take two or three to do the
job. In larger pieces of writing, such as books and theses,
it sometimes takes pages or even chapters to accommodate
each section of an outline. As a general rule, each section
of your draft will be roughly equal in length to all the others.

If the differences in length become really huge—say, by a factor of two or three—you are probably writing too much for the longer sections or, possibly, too little for the shorter ones. But this happens from time to time with first drafts; you can fix it later on, when you polish your product. This last section isn't too long compared with the previous ones, so let's barrel forward:

4. As for where this trend is going, we are heading for a time when all printed material will be available electronically, and when people with an interest in any particular subject or issue can communicate electronically to other people with the same interest, no matter where in the world they may be. This capability will accelerate the growth of human knowledge, as it becomes possible for everyone with new information, or new insights, to communicate what they have learned instantly and globally.

• Not much to say about what we did here, except that we expanded our outline by explaining just how the use of new telecommunications technologies will accelerate the growth of human knowledge. The reader may be a bit startled to read this, and we really ought to explain where this idea came from. Did one of the experts we talked with raise the point? Was it the focus of one of the articles we read? Or is it merely our own best judgment, based on everything we learned? We could stop right now, go back to the preceding section, and fix this up. Or we could do it later on, when we polish the first draft. It really doesn't matter, so long as the job gets done. Let's decide to roll forward and not break our momentum:

5. As for my own judgment, it seems clear that students with on-line access capabilities will be able to conduct research in wholly new and exciting ways. Working from their rooms they will be able to access libraries and other information sources throughout the world, easily and cheaply. The quality of their research will rise as students become familiar with these technologies. We ought to consider a course specifically designed to teach students how to take advantage of the telecommunications revolution.

- In this case we expanded our notes just a bit. Then we added a key recommendation of our own—namely, that a new course be developed.

And so, we have a first draft. To be sure, it needs more work before we'd actually want to show it to anybody. It's a bit vague in places, slightly repetitious here and there, sorely in need of a few more details and examples, and in general too "thin" for comfort. But that's all right. Remember, in a first draft we are more concerned with architecture than with execution. As we read through it once again, we see that we have in fact succeeded in following the course of our outline by expanding, beefing up, and fleshing out the outline's points and sections. Indeed, despite the draft's drawbacks and shortcomings its theme, its direction, and its overall thrust are sharp and clear. Thus we have accomplished our key first-draft objective.

Most professional writers consider this to be a major milestone. Reaching it usually brings on an intense feeling of relief and even a wave or two of euphoria. Writers have been known to celebrate this milestone by taking the rest of the day off, by treating themselves to a special lunch or dinner, by buying themselves a present of some sort or—in extreme cases—by going out and getting dead drunk. We don't recommend this last alternative, but we've been known to try the others ourselves and they are not bad at all. So, at least for a little while, let yourself go. After all, with a first draft on paper, or on your hard disk, the tough part is over.

And when you come back down to earth, you will be ready to go on to the third and final phase of the writing process, which is polishing your product. After running through the various skills and techniques required to turn your first draft into a finished product, we will return to the trend report we started and show how to carry it through to the end. You will be pleasantly surprised by how easy it will seem.

PART THREE

Polishing the Product

In this third and final part of the writing process—polishing the product—your objective is to enhance, sharpen, and focus your draft to give it power and credibility. After all, a piece of writing is successful only when it does what the writer intends it to do—for instance when the piece of writing informs, or persuades, or convinces, or when it stimulates the reader to take whatever action the writer wants him or her to take. And to be successful a piece of writing must earn the reader's respect through its internal power and credibility. You can impart these qualities to your own first draft—whether it be a memo, a letter, an article, a term paper, a book, or any other writing product—by complying with the nine key guidelines of draft-polishing:

- Be accurate
- Be precise
- Be consistent
- Be brief
- Be fair
- Keep a steady depth
- Keep a steady tone
- Use an established layout
- Use good grammar

In working your way through these guidelines, you will have more flexibility than you've had up to now. In the first two parts of the writing process, you operated like an architect and then an engineer, first designing and then constructing your product. So you had no choice but to use a step-by-step approach, because you literally had to complete one step before going on to the next step. But now that all the floors are laid down and the walls up, so to speak, you can operate more in the manner of an interior decorator. A decorator can work his way swiftly through all the rooms of a house, first putting in the furniture, then going back through all the rooms and hanging all the curtains, then going back again to install the lamps and once more for the appliances. Or, he can complete one room before going on to the next one.

You have the same choice of approaches for polishing your draft. In other words, there is no particular reason to work your way systematically through each successive section, never moving forward to the next section until you have applied all nine guidelines to whichever section you are working on. You can if you want to, of course. And many writers do. But if you prefer, you can move swiftly from one section to the next, applying just the first guideline to all the sections, then repeating the process over and over, each time applying another guideline, until you have applied all nine to the entire draft. It makes no difference at all which way you do it; it is entirely a matter of your own style and preference, as long as the job gets done.

Polishing the product, in addition to being the most flexible part of the writing process, is also the most variable part. It will either take the smallest chunk of your total time, or the largest chunk. It depends on three factors; the complexity of the piece you are writing, the thoroughness of the draft you've turned out, and the amount of time and energy you have got left when you reach this part. Obviously, the more complex the product you are writing, the more polishing you will need to do. For instance, a draft memo reminding people to attend a meeting next Thursday isn't going to need much polishing. But even a first-rate draft history of World War II is likely to require months or even years of effort to flesh out, refine, enhance. Moreover if you really skimmed your way through Parts One and Two, you are likely to find that there is a fair amount of work remaining to be done here in Part Three. On the other hand, if you took your time and did a careful, thorough job of organizing and drafting, much of what you would have needed to do in this third part you already will have done.

In all, polishing the product—rather like furnishing a new house that you have designed and built yourself—is often the most pleasant, satisfying part of the writing process. For this is when you bring it all together, when you enhance your draft and turn it into something that is finished, complete, effective, and uniquely your own. To be precise, what you do is this: you go over your draft—once, twice, or several times as you prefer—making additions, deletions, and modifications to comply as best you can with these key guidelines:

BE ACCURATE:

Nothing discredits a piece of writing faster, or more thoroughly, than a mistake which the reader notices. As you polish your draft, you must assume that your reader will know at least something about your subject; that he or she will know one fact, one name, one title, one place, one incident, one—something. And if you the writer get this "something" wrong, there is a high risk your reader will conclude that the entire piece of writing is riddled with mistakes that he or she just hasn't caught; that its author is lazy or incompetent and that the piece of writing itself should be given the absolute minimum attention or perhaps even dismissed outright. Unfortunately, there is no way for you, the writer, to predict which one fact, name, title, place, incident, or whatever your reader will know. So you have no choice but to put in sufficient time and energy to get all of them right.

There are two kinds of accuracy: accuracy of fact and accuracy of description.

Accuracy of fact requires more effort than brilliance. It is largely a matter of looking it up, checking it out, getting it straight. For example, if for some reason you are writing about the Declaration of Independence that created the United States, you need only spend a moment with any almanac or history book to be certain that the Declaration came in 1776. If you write that it happened in any other year, you will lose all credibility no matter how thorough and perceptive your account may be of the Declaration itself or of the American Revolution. Or, if you are writing up a report of a meeting, you had better not describe John Jones as the company's treasurer if in fact he's the general counsel. You say you're not sure which title is correct? Call the man's office and ask, or get hold of the company's annual report and look it up yourself. And if you are writing about a woman who has successfully launched her own business, for heaven's sake don't say it's a pet food company if in fact she's selling gourmet popcorn; don't describe her as tall if she's short, fat if she's thin, and the holder of an M.B.A. degree from the Harvard Business School if in fact she's a high-school dropout.

Check out facts yourself whenever possible. Get it wrong and the reader will hold you responsible, no matter where the fault really lies. If you write that the Declaration of Independence came in 1876, because that's what your sister's current boyfriend told you, you will have a mess on your hands. Not only won't your reader know who gave you wrong information, he or she won't care. You, and your piece of writing, will get the blame. Facts that can be checked out for certain must be checked out for certain. For example, the accuracy of every fact in this paragraph can be determined for certain by a writer:

The Happy Water Sailboat Company was founded in 1982 in Sag Harbor, New York. Sales during the first year of operation totaled $300,000, and doubled in 1984 to $600,000. The company now has sales offices in four locations throughout the region.

Of course, there are times when you do need to take somebody else's word for something. And at such times you protect yourself—that is, your own credibility and the credibility of whatever you are writing—by attributing facts that you cannot verify yourself directly to your source. For example:

According to Jenny Holmes, founder of the Happy Water Sailboat Company, the idea for the company emerged when friends in Sag Harbor told Ms. Holmes that they had tried to buy a boat that weekend and were disappointed to learn that there were no sailboat showrooms anywhere in the town. After making her own investigation of the situation and her own projections of potential sales the company was formed, according to Ms. Holmes.

If Ms. Holmes turns out to have a rotten memory or, worse, to be a liar, that's too bad for her. But you the writer are protected—provided that you have accurately reported whatever she has said or claimed. When in doubt about whether or not a fact should be attributed to a source other than yourself, as a general rule go ahead and make the attribution. Your source need not always be a person:

This year teachers in our school district will earn $30,000, according to Thursday's edition of The Daily Globe.

The company's annual report claims that six new products were offered to the public during the previous year.

Ownership of the house changed hands four times during the past decade, according to records in the county clerk's office.

Accuracy of description is every bit as important as accuracy of fact—but a bit trickier to achieve. In essence, when you describe an incident, an event, even a person, you have to get the sense of it right. For instance, let's say that for some reason you are writing about the US Space Shuttle program. Every single report of Space Shuttle blast-offs that has ever been written or recorded (even reports about the ill-fated *Challenger* mission) has described the crowds during count-down as tense, enthusiastic, fairly bursting with excitement. If your piece of writing uses words like "bored," "indifferent," and "complacent" to describe the count-down crowds — you are hopelessly off base. You haven't got the sense of right at all. You are just plain wrong. Likewise if you should describe the Lincoln Memorial in Washington D.C. as "unimpressive," or former President Ronald Reagan—whatever you may think of his policies, he is universally recognized as one of the world's most cheerful and optimistic leaders—as a sad-eyed, morose pessimist. You can't say these things; they are just not true.

Accuracy of description has nothing whatever to do with personal judgment and opinion. You are entitled to any views you wish about the US Space Shuttle program, the Lincoln Memorial, or about Ronald Reagan and the policies of his Administration, and of course you should express these views, if appropriate, in whatever you are writing. But when you are describing some thing, or some body, what you say must sound right to readers who have some idea of the truth, either from other pieces of writing, from other sources of information such as radio or television, or most importantly from their own personal experience.

It isn't always easy to "get the sense of it right." First, you must be careful to separate your personal judgment and opinion from the general perspective or recollection. For example, if you are writing up a report on a meeting of a university faculty that had been called to discuss whether students should be given the right to vote on their professors' requests for salary increases, you must set aside your own view of the issue long enough to report accurately how the meeting went. Did participants feel it was a good and useful meeting? Or did they consider it as a waste of time? Was the meeting harmonious or contentious? Was the mood angry? Cheerful? Businesslike? Sometimes you can "get the sense of it right" merely by staying alert during the proceedings. Other times you need to make an informal survey of participants.

Often it is just a matter of playing around with words and phrases until you find the ones that work best. Let's say you are trying to describe the taste of vanilla ice cream. Steer away from words like "delicious" and "awful," because these reflect personal opinion. Steer instead toward non-opinionated words like "smooth," "creamy," "cool," and "refreshing." In other words, you must scout around for words, or phrases, that describe accurately without also judging.

There is never any guarantee that a reader will accept your personal judgments and opinions. But you can be certain that if you fall short of total accuracy—both of fact and description—your readers will discredit whatever judgments and opinions you do express, however intelligent and valid they may be. So as you go about the business of polishing your draft keep in mind this rule: You are always entitled to your own judgments and opinions; you are never —never—entitled to your own facts. You must use the real ones, and you must get them right.

BE PRECISE:

Precision is a clear, direct reflection of how much effort a writer has devoted to his or her project. And because of this, readers tend to look kindly on pieces of writing that are consistently and visibly precise. By the same token, readers become uncomfortable and even downright snippy toward pieces of writing they judge to be imprecise. Fairly or not—and often without even realizing what they are doing—readers conclude that an imprecise writer has been lazy, and that the product itself isn't worth much attention. Simply put, then, the more precise your piece of writing is, the more willing your readers will be to accept or at least consider carefully your point of view. And you will be that much more likely to elicit from your readers the reaction or response that you want.

Precision is closely related to accuracy, but it is not quite the same thing. After all, you can be accurate but vague:

The first men to set foot on the moon landed there in the 1960s.

With a bit of effort you can be accurate and precise; with more effort you can be accurate and very precise;

The first men to set foot on the moon landed there in 1969.

The first men to set foot on the moon landed there on July 20, 1969.

Here's another set of examples, all accurate but each one more precise than the one before:

A senior official of the company voted against the chairman's proposal.

John Smith, a senior official of the company, voted against the chairman's proposal.

John Smith, executive vice president of the company, voted against the chairman's proposal.

John Smith, executive vice president of United Widget Corp., voted against the chairman's proposal.

John Smith, executive vice president of United Widget Corp., voted against the chairman's proposal to move corporate headquarters from Los Angeles to New York.

When you recount a concept, an idea, a program, a course of action—especially when it is someone else's—for the sake of your own credibility you must get the sense of it not only right, but precise. For example, this sentence is accurate but imprecise:

The mayor's program for reducing crime in the streets involves changes in the law itself and in the police department.

This is accurate and precise:

The mayor's program for reducing crime in the streets involves stiffer prison terms for convicted criminals and a 50 percent increase in the number of police officers assigned to neighborhood patrol duty.

Accurate:

The governor's anti-pollution program is a great success.

Accurate and precise:

The governor's anti-pollution program is a great success. Just two years after the program began, statistics show that our air and our water both are cleaner. According to the Committee For a Better Environment, at the present rate of improvement within three more years our air and water will be roughly twice as clean as they were before the program was launched.

As a general rule, readers want people that they read about to be identified with a high degree of precision—name, age, title if appropriate, home town:

John Harding, 45, chairman of Western Forge Company of Glendale, California, gave the keynote speech.

Police said the bank was robbed by Judy Caldwell, 34, an unemployed radio announcer from New York City.

You should identify a person only once, and you should always do it the first time that he or she is mentioned. After that, it is sufficient to use just the person's name. However, since people are curious about other people, it's always a good idea to offer your readers additional little tidbits of information whenever it is convenient and appropriate to do so. For instance, let's say that you are writing a newspaper article about a scholarship winner. The first time you mention this individual you would give just these key details:

Jimmy Johnson, 17, a senior at Western High School in Oak Grove, Louisiana, won a full scholarship to Harvard University.

But the next time you mention Jimmy Johnson, you could use the occasion to slip in an extra tidbit:

Johnson, who works on Saturday afternoons in his father's hardware store on Main Street, said Thursday that he plans to study biology.

If the extra tidbits you've slipped in seem all right, then let them remain in the text. But if you read through your text a second time and you decide you've put in too much information, go ahead and take some out. There are no hard and fast rules to cover this; your own judgment is really the best guide.

When describing concepts, ideas, proposed courses of action, and so forth, you must give enough information so that the reader can get a clear idea of what's involved. Moreover, by spelling out with precision a concept, an idea, or a proposed course of action, it becomes apparent to the reader that you—the writer—have devoted sufficient effort to know what you are talking about. And this, of course, helps to establish and maintain your own credibility:

> *The country has two political parties, the Yellows and the Blues. The Blues' program for reducing poverty rests primarily on use of the tax structure to transfer wealth from richer citizens to poorer citizens. More precisely, the Blues would raise taxes for families with incomes of $50,000 a year or more, then transfer this money to families with incomes of less than $50,000 a year through an assortment of social spending measures such as welfare payments and food stamps. The Blues haven't specified the amount of the middle-income and upper-income tax hikes that they would enact.*

Or:

> *The Yellows' program for reducing poverty rests primarily on the idea of lowering taxes for everyone, and by doing so to trigger higher rates of economic growth. More precisely, the Yellows would cut taxes for all citizens by a total of 30 percent over a three-year period, in hopes that people would both consume and invest the additional money in ways that would create new jobs and thus trigger a higher growth rate. This, in turn, would reduce the need for the social-spending measures, such as welfare payments and food stamps, that the Blues are advocating.*

As you can see, once you get the hang of being precise there is almost no limit to the level of precision you can achieve. Obviously, you will need to apply some judgment. On the one hand, you never want to be too vague. On the other hand, you don't want to waste three pages describing a doorknob. In the majority of cases, you can achieve the right level of precision simply by following these two rules: First, be certain to give your reader enough detailed information to convince him or her that you, the writer, have done your homework and know what you are talking about. Second, put yourself in the reader's place and ask: What would I need to know about this person, this event, this idea, this program, this course of action, or whatever? What would I want to know? When the level of precision satisfies you, so too will it satisfy your readers.

BE CONSISTENT:

You can not expect to help somebody else make up his or her mind about something if you have not yet made up your own. So throughout your piece of writing, both your personal judgments and your descriptions—of people, of events, of ideas—must be internally consistent.

Judgments and descriptions that are mutually exclusive are not tolerable in any piece of writing. If in your first paragraph you describe an individual as "willful," you must be careful not to describe him or her three paragraphs later as "weak-minded." A house that is "beautiful" on the first page of your letter to Aunt Tilly cannot become a "hideous" or "ugly" house on page two. An event that is "exciting" at one point in your piece of writing cannot be "boring" in another. And a "revolutionary" idea at the beginning of your piece of writing cannot become a "long-standing, discredited" idea at the end.

Once again, the solution is to think before you write. Don't just leap on the first descriptive word that comes to mind. Give careful thought to your own perceptions of people, of events, of ideas. Reach your judgments slowly and carefully. But when you do reach them, stick to them all the way. If you read through a draft you've written and find conflicting judgments—that is, judgments that are not

merely different, but mutually exclusive—you should realize what lies behind the problem. Namely, that you the
writer have not yet made up your own mind or, worse, that
you hold mutually exclusive views about something and
simply haven't realized it. Ultimately, the solution is easy;
you change one of the judgments or descriptions. But don't
do it too quickly. First, stop to think about which judgment
or description you really want; about which one truly
reflects your own perception or point of view.

BE BRIEF:

Back in the nineteenth century—before television,
before video tape recorders, before Nintendo—families
entertained themselves by reading aloud to one another.
Naturally there was a huge appetite for reading material,
and in England writers like Charles Dickens were hired by
newspapers and magazines to spin out their stories in
lengthy episodes that stretched across weeks and months.
Since the objective was to help readers kill time, the longer
the episodes the better. Dickens was actually paid according to the number of column inches his work took up when
published.

We live in a very different world. To be sure, reading
the classics will always be among the greatest pleasures a
civilized person can enjoy. But people don't have much
time any more to read for pleasure. Most of the reading that
most people do today is required reading. That is, people
read mostly because they have to; because they need to
absorb information. Indeed, this is the kind of reader we've
been focusing on here in *How to Write*.

But what about those assignments back in high school
or college, where you were required to write 5,000-word
essays on such-and-such and your entire focus and effort
were on spinning out a piece of writing that met the required
length? Our answer is: forget it. Assigning long essays on

sophisticated literary concepts is a terrible way to teach writing. It may have forced you to read and think more about a given topic than you otherwise would have done. But it didn't teach you to communicate ideas and information clearly and concisely. In fact, it may well have gotten you into the habit of blathering on just to fill up space.

When you are writing for someone who will read your product because he or she needs to read it, you want to take up as little of your reader's time and energy as necessary to do the job properly. In other words, you want to be brief.

The trick to being brief is to be utterly ruthless with yourself and with your draft. First, read through your draft and take out anything that is repetitious. Make your points well, but never make the same point twice. If you've fallen in love with the way you made a point the second time, stick with that formulation and eliminate the first one. Choose. Then read through your draft again to see if you've included the same fact twice. If you have, decide which place is best to include that fact and get rid of the other place.

Second, eliminate anything from your draft that is not directly relevant to your objective. This is often a painful thing to do, because "diversions" are often the most enjoyable and interesting parts of a draft. For example, if you are sending your boss a trip report on your meeting with an accounting firm in St. Louis, don't tell him about the movie star you sat next to on the airplane. At least, don't tell him in your report; tell him about it the next time you and he are chatting at the water cooler. Keep your piece of writing on course at all times; save the detours for another day.

Curiously enough, it takes more effort to be brief than it does to ramble on. As the American humorist Ambrose Bierce once scribbled at the end of a letter to a friend, "Forgive me for writing such a long letter. I didn't have time to write a short one." And it isn't just the effort. It's the pain. Time and again you will find yourself removing good stuff not because it isn't good enough, but because it just doesn't belong there. This hurts, but you must force yourself to do it. Keep in mind that your reader will never know what you removed from your draft. All the reader knows is what ends up in the final product, and the less time and energy your reader needs to cope with that product the more likely you will be to achieve your objective.

BE FAIR:

Fairness in a person is admirable; in a piece of writing it is essential. That's because the absence of fairness stands out very clearly when you write; indeed it stands out far more clearly than when you speak. This is why the sort of flippant, off-hand comments you can get away with when you speak you simply cannot make when you write. For instance, you can get away with calling someone a horse-thief in a conversation; do it in writing and you're in trouble —unless the individual literally has been convicted in a court of stealing a horse. Likewise, in a casual conversation you can brush off an idea you don't like as "dumb" or "stupid." In a piece of writing you would need to analyze the idea so that, in the end, your reader would come to understand why the idea is flawed or unworkable. In short, the standards for writing are much more strict than the standards for speaking. If the reader judges what you write to be unfair—it doesn't matter whether in fact this is a reasonable judgment; it matters only that the reader reaches this judgment—your ability is diminished to inform, to influence, to persuade, or to convince.

Being fair means including relevant facts even when they don't support the point you want to make. After all, you can support any point at all, no matter how vicious or idiotic, merely by including only those facts that support the point you want to make and leaving out everything else. For example:

The United States is an evil country. Twice in this century, it has fought in World Wars.

Even when the point you want to make is reasonable and perfectly valid, it's a rare instance when all the relevant facts support your point. Often you can gain credibility by acknowledging evidence or conditions that, so to speak, go in the wrong direction:

Washington D.C. is a lovely city in which to live. The buildings are beautiful, the residential neighborhoods are pleasant, and shopping is convenient. However, summers in Washington are unbearable, as temperatures hover above 90 degrees with tropical-type humidity.

Or:

In sum, then, moving our headquarters from Manhattan out to suburban Westchester County will have several advantages. Our office rental costs would be lower, our employees, most of whom live in Westchester now, would have shorter commutes to work, we would be closer to our markets in New England, and local tax rates would be lower than in Manhattan. On the other hand, by leaving New York City we would distance ourselves from our three prime competitors, all of whom are in Manhattan. Thus it would be harder for us to know what they are up to. Moreover, since many of our sales executives will need to visit New York customers regularly, they would need to spend quite a bit of time traveling back and forth from Manhattan to our headquarters in Westchester County.

Never be afraid to include a relevant fact just because it doesn't support your argument. As long as your argument is sound, and as long as you include all the necessary facts to show your reader that it's sound, there is no danger that your reader will suddenly turn on you. Indeed, the danger is that your reader will discover the contrary fact by himself or herself—and will wonder how come it never occurred to you. Remember, you can never be certain that your piece of writing is the only piece your reader will read before making up his or her mind. In essence, when you write you want not simply to tell your reader *what* to think about a subject, but rather you want to show your reader *how* to think about a subject. You want to show all the facts that you took into account—and which, therefore, your reader should take into account—in reaching your own conclusions.

Being fair also means reporting the existence of opinions other than your own. This is an especially vital thing to do when your judgment or opinion is unique or at least uncommon:

> *War and Peace is the most boring novel I have ever read. It's much too long, the author goes on for page after page describing things of absolutely no interest, and of the dozens of characters in the book there is not one that I find attractive or sympathetic. To be sure, War and Peace is widely acclaimed as one of the greatest novels of all time, largely because of its historic sweep and what many critics consider the overwhelming power of its prose. But in my view the novel's drawbacks exceed its strengths.*

Or:

> *I have decided to end our system of assigned parking places. I realize that most of you like the present system, on the grounds that each of you knows where his parking space will be no matter what time you arrive for work, and that you therefore oppose this change. But after due consideration I remain convinced that a first-come, first-served parking space system will be more fair and more efficient since it will reward those who arrive early and penalize those who show up late.*

Your readers will find a unique or unpopular opinion or decision much easier to take if you acknowledge its uniqueness or unpopularity. Doing so suggests that you have considered the alternatives, and have decided to stick with your opinion or go ahead with your decision anyway. This implies conviction, which in turn earns credibility.

Finally, being fair means taking circumstances into account. Remember, when you write you are the eyes and ears of your reader. He or she is relying on you, through your piece of writing, to present a balanced picture or point of view:

Bill Harper's presentation to our Civic Improvement Society was not as sharply focused as we had hoped. Moreover, during the question-and-answer session after his presentation Bill was curt and even rude to some members of the audience. In sum, we were extremely disappointed and more than a little angry. To be sure, we later learned that one of Bill's children had entered the hospital just that morning; this may well have accounted for Bill's performance.

Of course, being fair does not invariably mean you must excuse everything or everyone you criticize. Take out the final sentence of the above paragraph, facts permitting, and with this substitution the paragraph would end with a very different tone:

This is not the first time Bill has performed in an unsatisfactory manner. I've checked with several people who attended his last three presentations, and they all report that Bill seemed unprepared, and that he was curt and rude to members of his audiences. Moreover, there are no special circumstances that I can find to explain this away. Clearly, then, Bill's latest performance is part of an inexcusable trend.

Again, being fair does not mean being kind, or agreeing with every imaginable opinion or point of view. It simply means taking circumstances into account and re-porting these circumstances to your reader so that he or she can see that your judgments are based on a genuine under-standing of the situation or the issue.

Always keep in mind how important it is to earn and keep your reader's respect—and how easy it is to lose this respect by not being fair. When you find yourself reluctant to include a relevant fact you know that fairness requires be included—and this happens to every writer now and then—it usually means your argument is weak or otherwise badly flawed and that deep down you know it. The solution is not to fight the problem or to ignore it, but rather to face the problem and deal with it.

KEEP A STEADY DEPTH:

Imagine walking into an electronics store in search of some equipment for your home. As you browse through the displays, you discover that the store offers twenty models of videotape recorders, twenty-five different television sets, about the same number of CD players—and one model telephone answering machine. This would seem odd, to say the least. After all, we expect a store to maintain a certain balance in its stock of merchandise. So too with pieces of writing, and in writing this balance of merchandise that we expect is called depth.

All pieces of writing have a certain depth. One difference between good and bad pieces of writing is that in good pieces, the depth holds steady all the way through. A bad piece of writing is one in which the depth fluctuates. For example, a book on US history during the twentieth century that has two hundred pages about World War I and two hundred pages about the Great Depression, should not have just five pages about World War II.

Choosing the proper depth for your piece of writing is among the key decisions you need to make. There is no rule

for doing this, except the obvious: you give your reader as
much detail as necessary to accomplish your ends. Instinct
and common sense usually do the trick. The problem tends
to show up somewhere in the middle of a draft, when for
some reason the writer changes depth either by going
deeper—giving too much detail about a particular incident,
point, person, idea—or by rising up to a more shallow depth
—which is to say giving too few details about a particular
incident, point, person, idea. It isn't that one depth is
necessarily better than the other; it is the very fact of the
change that unsettles the reader. For example:

*Present at the meeting were John Smith, a teacher
from Akron, Ohio; Hazel Hawkins, a chemical engineer
from Tallahassee, Florida; Gerald Williams, an electrician
from Rochester, New York; and Howard Snelling, 45, a
lawyer from San Francisco who is a graduate of Yale
University, served for three years as a lieutenant in the US
Marine Corps, spent twelve years with the Global Construction Company, and who in 1992 placed third in the
Boston Marathon.*

It is just as unsettling to a reader when the depth of a
piece of writing changes in the opposite direction. That is,
when it suddenly rises up to a more shallow level:

*In sum, there are three houses in this neighborhood
suitable for your family and within the price range you have
selected. The first is a three-bedroom brick town house on
Oak Street, built in 1965 with gas heating and central air
conditioning. Its kitchen has just been remodeled, all the
rooms have wall-to-wall carpeting, and local taxes are
$1,500 a year. The second house is a four-bedroom
colonial on Elm Street, built of wood and aluminum siding
in 1963. It uses oil heat, has four room air conditioners, a
large family room downstairs, and an apartment with a
separate entrance that is currently rented for $200 per*

month. Local taxes last year totaled $1,200. The third
possibility is a ranch house.

In lengthy pieces of writing, you hold a steady depth all the way through by giving equal weight to facts, events, people, and ideas that are equally important to whatever you are writing. For instance, in a book about World War II you would certainly need to talk about World War I and the Great Depression, since each was among the causes of the latter conflict. But you would not need to discuss World War I and the Great Depression in the same detail as you would need to discuss the book's main subject, World War II. However, you would discuss World War I and the Great Depression in equal detail to each other, if you are contending that each contributed equally to World War II. And within your discussion of World War II, you would give equal treatment to battles that you judge to be equally significant.

Different writers have different approaches to this need for setting and holding a steady depth. Some turn out first drafts that, in general, have far too much depth. Others turn out first drafts that, in general, are too shallow. When polishing their drafts, those writers in the first category find themselves removing details here and there, while those in the second category find themselves adding details here and there. Neither approach is necessarily better than the other; as so often is the case, it is merely a question of personal style. All that matters is that at some point during the writing process you select an appropriate depth and then hold it steady all the way through.

KEEP A STEADY TONE:

So similar is the tone issue to the depth issues that you could re-read the preceding section, substituting tone for depth, and have it just about right. Very briefly then, every piece of writing has a tone: serious, flippant, formal, informal, aggressive, friendly, forceful, gentle, nasty, cheerful, and so forth. You can choose whatever tone you want — whichever one you find most appropriate, most comfortable, and which you believe will achieve the goals of your particular piece of writing. But once you make this choice, you must stick with it all the way through. You cannot change your mind—that is, your tone—in the middle. A change of tone is as easy to recognize as a change of depth:

Dear Representative Holden,

I am writing to protest your vote last Thursday, in which you opposed the President's defense budget. I believe a strong defense is absolutely vital to protect our national security, and it is because the President shares this view that I have supported him throughout his Administration. Your vote against higher defense spending will encourage our nation's enemies to believe that we no longer have the will to defend our society. Thus I urge you to reconsider your position on this important issue. Should you hold to your present position, I cannot guarantee my support in your next election. Besides, your speech on this subject was a real stinker; I don't know how you can say such garbage. Maybe you're crazy.

Or:

Dear Joe;

Are you crazy? Why in heaven's name did you vote against the President's defense bill last Thursday? You know as well as I do that a strong defense is absolutely vital to our national security. Besides, votes like yours only encourage potential enemies to think they can walk all over us. And Joe, that speech of yours was a real stinker. Do us both a favor and give this issue some more thought. How-

ever, in the event that you choose to persist with your present line of voting, I must warn you that neither I nor my family will support you in your next election campaign. I trust, therefore, that you will take this matter under careful advisement.

Choosing the right tone in the first place is fairly easy. It requires merely that you have some sense of occasion. That is, use precisely the tone you would use if you were talking to the individual who will be your reader. The better you know the intended reader—and the better the reader knows you—the less formal you likely will be. Of course, in many pieces of writing you will choose a tone that is really a combination of tones: friendly but furious, formal but cheerful, dignified but indignant, and so forth. Use whatever tone makes you comfortable; your instinct will nearly always be good. Just read through your first draft to see what tone you have in fact selected. If it strikes you as the wrong tone, change it immediately. If you are comfortable with the tone you have chosen, as you polish your draft just make certain to hold that tone all the way through.

USE AN ESTABLISHED LAYOUT:

In writing, as in everything else, presentation matters hugely. Present something well, and its merits become more visible than its flaws. Present something badly, and its weaknesses show up more clearly than its strengths. In writing, the technical word for presentation is "layout." It simply means the physical design and appearance of your product.

There are no ironclad laws that govern the layouts for pieces of writing in all the different categories—sales brochures, technical papers, book reviews, letters of inquiry or complaint, newspaper and magazine articles, notices to employees, reports of meetings, high school themes, college essays, how-to books, and so forth. Nor are there any hard-and-fast rules that dictate the size or color of paper to use, the typeface style, the correct width of lines or numbers of lines per page, or, for instance whether to put the date on a letter you are writing at the top of the page or at the bottom, against the left margin or against the right.

But there is no need to design from scratch your own layout for whatever you are writing. For one thing, the choice of layout very often does not belong to the writer. After all, when you submit something for publication in a newspaper or magazine, it isn't you the writer but the editor who needs to choose a layout. All you the writer need do is send in your finished, polished piece of writing in a clear, legible form. You really don't have any layout decisions to make at all.

But even when you the writer are submitting the finished product without an editor or middleman of some sort to handle the layout—for example when you are writing a letter, or a memo, or an essay of some sort for school—there is no need to design a layout from scratch. For no matter what category your own piece of writing falls into, it is a category that has been around for a long time, and one for which through trial and error effective layouts have long since been established.

This is one time when it makes good sense to take the easy way out. Literally get your hands on several pieces of writing in your category that have already been done by other people. For instance, if you are writing a letter requesting a job interview, get your hands on some job-interview letters that other people have written. Or if you are writing up a report on this week's meeting of the annual picnic committee, ask around to see if the report on last week's meeting is available, of if the files from last year's venture are still around. You should not be the slightest bit embarrassed to do this. First, it makes sense and doing the sensible thing is never wrong. Second, you can bet your life that the people who wrote the examples you are collecting themselves did precisely the same thing. Don't you think we went around to libraries and bookstores, browsing through and buying up all sorts of "how-to" books, before deciding on the layout for this one? Of course we did; we would have been foolish not to have done so.

Happily, for a growing number of writing categories, very specific "how-to" books and pamphlets are now available in most libraries and bookstores. You can find books and pamphlets devoted exclusively to the subjects of how to write resumes, business letters, technical papers, doctoral theses, and all sorts of writing categories. While the quality of these books and pamphlets varies, most provide excellent illustrative examples of the most effective, established layouts for their respective categories. These books and pamphlets will be especially useful if you aren't able to put your hands on "real" examples.

Again, there are no ironclad laws, no hard-and-fast rules. So in theory, you can design any layout you want. But the established layouts work; that's why they have become established. So go ahead and collect some examples, browse through them, and when you find the one that seems most comfortable to you and most effective for the piece you are writing and for the reader you have in mind—simply duplicate the layout.

Or if you prefer, use today's software to help out. In just the last few years a number of software packages have reached the market that generate standard layouts for all sorts of standard categories of writing, such as resumes, business plans and annual reports. By all means check out these products at your local software store. If you find one that appeals to you, don't hesitate for a moment to buy the software, to install it and to use it regularly.

USE GOOD GRAMMAR:

You were probably beginning to think that we were going to make it all the way to the end of this book without once mentioning the most dreaded word in all the world of writing: grammar. Well, sorry but here we go. Grammar—which means the proper use of words and punctuation to construct sentences—is important. In any language, the established rules of grammar make it easier to communicate precisely because these rules are established, which is to say they are widely accepted and understood. Obviously, the better your own command of these rules—your command of grammar—the easier it is for others to grasp your point. Can you communicate without total or near-total command of your language's grammar? Of course you can, and people do. But it's harder—that is, it requires more effort by those you are communicating with—and so your ability to communicate effectively is diminished. Put another way, the weaker your grammar the greater the burden on your reader to grasp your point. And the harder it is for someone to grasp your point, the less likely you are to succeed—that is, to effectively communicate your ideas and information—no matter how good your point may be.

There is no language in the world whose rules of grammar are too hard for the overwhelming majority of people to learn. After all, everybody learns to talk well enough to communicate. And the rules of grammar that apply to speech are precisely the same as those for writing. The only difference, as we have said before, is that for obvious reasons grammatical errors show up more starkly in writing than in speaking. So the need to be correct when you write is greater than the need to be correct when you speak. This explains why most schools in most countries, when they teach writing, put so much emphasis on teaching the rules of grammar. In theory, then, by the time you finish high school you should know the rules of grammar in your language. After all, you already knew how to talk when you arrived at kindergarten.

Nevertheless, if you don't have a firm grip on the rules of grammar now—when you need to write something—you have a problem that must be solved quickly. It would take a book ten times the size of this one to sketch out all the rules of grammar, to give examples, and to explain all the tricky details well enough to give you a firm grip on the subject. Happily, dozens of such books are easily available, and you should get your hands on one immediately if poor grammar is your special problem. In addition, today's software products can help here, too. There is software to check your spelling, to measure the length of sentences and highlight those which are too long, to signal potential errors of syntax or style. The quality of these products varies, although generally they are getting better all the time. Once again, if you find a software product that works for you, go right ahead and use it.

Whether or not you use software or a grammar book—or both—checking your piece of writing for grammatical errors should always be the very last thing you do before sending your finished product on its way to your intended reader or readers. The chances are that you, like most people, use better grammar when you talk than when you write. One trick to catching grammatical errors in your writing product is simply to read the piece out loud, as though you were talking it out to your reader. If something suddenly sounds off-key, it's a good bet you have found a grammatical error. If you can see how to fix it, go ahead. If you can't see how to fix it, consult whatever software program or grammar book you are using. Or, in a pinch, ask a friend or colleague for help. Again, don't be embarrassed to ask for help; you will be more embarrassed if your product goes forward with a grammatical mistake in it.

As you can see from all these guidelines, polishing your product requires a combination of judgment and applied technique. Your objective is to smooth out the rough edges, fill in the cracks, bolster weak sections and generally balance the whole product so that your reader will find it easy to absorb your ideas and information and, ultimately, your point. How you do all this is your business, dependent wholly on your style and taste. You can apply one guideline to all the sections of your draft, then start from the beginning again with the second guideline then again with the third, fourth, and so on. Or you can apply all the guidelines to the first section, going on to the second section only when the first is fully polished, then so on through all the subsequent sections of your draft. Keep in mind, of course, that in most cases you won't need to modify each section to accommodate all the guidelines. In all likelihood, you will have only one or two flaws in each draft section. That is, Section One might need more precision and better grammar, while Section Two will need a touch of accuracy and Section Four will have a depth or tone problem.

To show you just what all this really looks like, let's go back to our draft of **The On-Line Research Revolution**. First, we will repeat the draft of each section exactly as it appears in Part Two. Then we will write out a polished version of this same section. We will follow this, in turn, with an explanation of why we made each change in the first draft—of which particular guideline led us to make each particular change in the text. We will repeat this one-two-three pattern for each section, so you can really see how to polish a draft and what a finished product looks like. Mostly in the interest of saving space—but also because it suits our own style and taste—we'll use the second approach to draft-polishing. That is, we will apply all the guidelines to each section before going on to the next one:

THEME

Draft Version:

A telecommunications revolution is under way in which people are using computers to access information through telephone lines. By doing so people can connect electronically to libraries, data bases, bulletin board systems and other such on-line sources to acquire information on virtually any subject, at a very low cost. The trend is moving swiftly, and in a few years virtually all printed information will be available electronically. This is a good trend that will enable students to conduct research more effectively and efficiently.

Polished Version:

A telecommunications revolution is under way in which people are using computers to access information through telephone lines. By doing so people can connect electronically to libraries, data bases, bulletin board systems and other such on-line sources to acquire information on virtually any subject, at a very low cost. The trend is moving swiftly, and in a few years virtually all printed information will be available electronically. This is a good trend that will enable students to conduct research more effectively and efficiently.

Reasons for Changes:

As you can see, we made no changes at all. This isn't surprising, because we fussed a great deal with our theme when we drafted it. It had to be just right, so we honed it several times even before we made our outline. As a general rule, you hone a theme so carefully when you draft it that little if any polishing is ever needed. It's the succeeding sections that need most of the polishing for accuracy, precision, consistency, fairness, and so forth. So as you read through your theme when you settle down to polish your draft, just make certain that the grammar is correct. Save your polishing efforts for what follows.

SECTION ONE

Draft Version:

A *telecommunications revolution is under way, in which people are using their computers in new ways to access information through telephone lines. So much information is now available electronically that this constitutes a new form of media, one that is changing the very nature of research.*

Polished Version:

Today much of the information that used to be available only in printed form is now available electronically as well. According to the university's Chief Librarian, Cynthia Jones, this includes newspapers, magazines, books, and encyclopedias. So much information is now available electronically that this constitutes a new form of media that is changing the very nature of research by making much more information available to people than they could find in their local libraries.

Reasons for Changes:

1. For the sake of being brief, we took out the first sentence; it was just a repeat of the first sentence we used in our theme.

2. To build in more precision, we described the kinds of printed materials—newspapers, magazines, books and encyclopedias—that are now available electronically.

3. For accuracy's sake we attributed these details to our source, the university's Chief Librarian, Cynthia Jones.

SECTION TWO

Draft Version:

New technologies that enable computers and tele-phones to work together are fueling the trend. More precisely, anyone with a modem-equipped computer can "dial up" to a wide range of electronic information sources such as libraries, data bases and bulletin board systems. These sources generally charge modest hourly fees, and in some cases extra fees for access to certain information or for the right to print out information or to "download" it onto one's own computer.

Polished Version:

New technologies that enable computers and tele-phones to work together are fueling the trend. The key technology here is called a modem, and it is an electronic device that transmits data, rather than voice, through a telephone line. Thus anyone with a modem-equipped com-puter can "dial up" to a wide range of electronic informa-tion sources such as libraries, data bases and bulletin board systems to receive information. These sources gen-erally charge modest hourly fees, ranging from $6.95 to $30, and in some cases extra fees for access to certain information or for the right to print out information or to "download" it onto one's own computer.

Reasons for Changes:

1. We added a new second sentence here to explain just what the new technology is that's fueling the trend; this makes our section both more accurate and more precise.

2. Once again, to add precision we provided specific figures for the hourly access fees that, in the first draft, we only described as "modest."

SECTION THREE

Draft Version:

Companies are springing up all over the country that provide information electronically. Some of these companies offer what amount to electronic versions of libraries from which books, articles and even software products can be read and "downloaded." Other companies are setting up bulletin board systems, which are a form of electronic meeting place where people with a shared interest can exchange ideas and information. For instance, there are bulletin boards for people interested in business, education, cooking, music and even some television shows such as **Star Trek**. The **Star Trek** bulletin board has separate sections for each of the shows' characters, such as Captain Kirk and Captain Picard, and even one section to focus on the efforts of Mr. Data to become human.

At the same time, telephone companies are upgrading their lines to carry the increasing flow of data. They are even preparing for a time when video can be transmitted over these lines onto computers. And the computer makers are starting to get their act together by developing the technologies that will enable computers to function like televisions.

Polished Version:

Companies are springing up all over the country that provide information electronically. Some of these companies offer what amount to electronic versions of libraries from which books, articles and even software products can be read and "downloaded." Other companies are setting up bulletin board systems, which are a form of electronic meeting place where people with a shared interest can exchange ideas and information. For instance, there are bulletin boards for people interested in business, educa-

*tion, cooking, music and even some television shows such as **Star Trek**. The **Star Trek** bulletin board has separate sections for each of the shows' characters, such as Captain Kirk and Captain Picard, and even one section to focus on the efforts of Mr. Data to become human.*

At the same time, telephone companies are upgrading their lines to carry the increasing flow of data. They are even preparing for a time when video can be transmitted over these lines onto computers. And the computer makers are working now to develop the technologies that will enable computers to function like televisions.

Reasons for Changes:

1. We only made one change in this entire section, but it was an important one. In the last sentence of the second paragraph, referring to the computer makers, we took out the phrase *"starting to get their act together by developing the technologies"* and substituted the phrase *"working now to develop the technologies."* The draft sentence projects a very different tone from the rest of the trend report; a tone much more suitable to two students chatting over lunch than to a report from one professional to his supervisor. The polished phrase is more appropriate; it reflects the informal but dignified tone we chose at the start.

SECTION FOUR

Draft Version:

As for where this trend is going, we are heading for a time when all printed material will be available electronically, and when people with an interest in any particular subject or issue can communicate electronically to other people with the same interest, no matter where in the world they may be. This capability will accelerate the growth of human knowledge, as it becomes possible for everyone with new information, or new insights, to communicate what they have learned instantly and globally.

Polished Version:

We are heading for a time when all printed material will be available electronically, and when people with an interest in any particular subject or issue can communicate electronically with other people who share the same interest, no matter where in the world they may be. This capability will accelerate the growth of human knowledge, as it becomes possible for everyone with new information, or new insights, to communicate what they have learned instantly and globally. For example, a physician who discovers a new way to treat bronchitis can pass on his discovery not merely to his local colleagues but to physicians all over the world by going "on-line" to a doctor's bulletin board and posting a message.

Reasons for Changes:

1. For brevity's sake, we got rid of the opening phrase, *"As for where this trend is going ...."* It just isn't necessary.

2. Further along, we added a sentence: *For example, a physician who discovers a new way to treat bronchitis can pass on his discovery not merely to his local colleagues but to physicians all over the world by going "on-line" to a doctor's bulletin board and posting a message.* This adds considerable precision to the point by giving the reader a real example of just how the on-line revolution will work.

SECTION FIVE

Draft Version:

As for my own judgment, it seems clear that with on-line access capabilities students will be able to conduct research in wholly new and exciting ways. Working from their rooms they will be able to access libraries and other information sources throughout the world, easily and cheaply. The quality of their research will rise as students become familiar with these technologies. We ought to consider a course specifically designed to teach students how to take advantage of the telecommunications revolution.

Polished Version:

As for my own judgment, it seems clear that with on-line access capabilities students will be able to conduct research in wholly new and exciting ways. Working from their rooms they will be able to access libraries and other information sources throughout the world, easily and cheaply. The quality of their research will rise as students become familiar with these technologies. To be sure, on-line access capability by itself does not guaranty better quality research. The skills and techniques of doing research—of reading through information and sifting it for ideas and insights—remain the same whether the information is in printed or electronic form. If students aren't taught these skills and techniques they will not do high-quality research no matter how advanced the technologies they utilize. Nevertheless, students with good research skills and techniques will be helped enormously by these new technologies. On balance, then, we ought to consider a course specifically designed to teach students how to take advantage of the telecommunications revolution.

Reasons for Changes:

We made one very big change here -- the inclusion of four new sentences: *To be sure, on-line access capability by itself does not guaranty better quality research. The skills and techniques of doing research -- of reading through information and sifting it for ideas and insights -- remain the same whether the information is in printed or electronic form. If students aren't taught these skills and techniques they will not do high-quality research no matter how advanced the technologies they utilize. Nevertheless, students with good research skills and techniques will be helped enormously by these new technologies.* We included these sentences to be fair—to present the other side of the argument. We wanted our reader to know that we had thought seriously about the theme of our trend report and that we understood it thoroughly. And these four sentences required us to slightly modify the last sentence by adding the phrase, *"On balance ..."*.

As you can see, polishing our draft was quite a project. Once we got past our theme, we made at least one change in each section. Interestingly, nearly half our changes were made to accommodate the same guideline: Be precise. That's because our own style is to move briskly through a draft, turning out one that is rather on the thin side. So we always need to flesh out and beef up our drafts, and we do that by making our general statements or assertions more precise. Other writers tend to "over-write". That is, they turn out drafts that are much too long and too detailed. Their primary polishing chore is to thin out their drafts by cutting them down to size. As we said earlier, it doesn't matter how you prefer to work, as long as the polished product comes out properly.

Like most writers, we are never quite satisfied with our work. We always want to make one more change, and as long as time permits there is no reason not to go over a polished draft one more time. We have just done that—and we've found something we should have seen earlier. Look at the last sentence of the first paragraph in Section Three, as it appears after polishing: *The **Star Trek** bulletin board has separate sections for each of the shows' characters, such as Captain Kirk and Captain Picard, and even one section to focus on the efforts of Mr. Data to become human.* We're embarrassed to admit it, but by including this section we changed our depth rather drastically. We gave much too much information abut one particular bulletin board and on second glance—actually, on third glance—we realized what we had done. The solution is simple: we could end the sentence after the word *"characters"* or we could eliminate the entire sentence. Either choice would work, and we choose the latter.

Now that we have gone through all the sections of our draft, and polished them as best we can, the next step is to make certain that our product fits into an established layout. In this case, we would take a look at some other trend reports that we have managed to get our hands on. If one of these reports has a layout that seems appropriate, we could use this same layout for our report. Or, we might have a software package on our hard drive that formats trend reports. If so, we would go ahead and use that layout. Finally, we would run our report through the spellchecker that comes with our word processing package, then hit the print button and turn out a final copy.

There is just one more step to take before we are done. If at all possible, when we have a "final" copy in our hands we should literally walk away from it. We should get a cup of coffee or a glass of milk, take a walk around the block, go for a jog or a bike ride, call on our friends or play with our children—anything that will help us to relax and clear our minds. We have just been through an arduous process, one that is difficult and draining even for the most experienced, professional writers. Then, when we are feeling up to it, we will take one more "final" look at our product. If we can see something that needs fixing—a misspelled word here, a grammatical error there, a poorly written phrase somewhere else, a missing example or even one example too many—we will go ahead and make the necessary change, then print out the real "final" version.

But that's it. We will have reached the point of diminishing returns, and any changes we make after that would be just as likely to weaken our piece of writing as to strengthen it. We must accept the fact that with more time, and more experience, we could have done better. But we have done the best we can, and we've done it by working in an orderly, sensible fashion. Now it is time to send our piece of writing forward to its intended reader.

We have worked our way through the process outlined here in *How to Write*, so our reader should have no difficulty whatever grasping what we mean to say. And enabling the reader to grasp our meaning is what matters most.

Ready, Set, Go

As we said at the outset, *How to Write* is a handbook. So keep it handy, and use it to guide yourself through whatever it is you need to write. Above all, remember that writing is a process. So don't be surprised—or disappointed—if some or even all the steps we have outlined in Parts One, Two and Three seem awkward or difficult your first time out. All processes take a bit of time and experience to master. After you have worked your way through one or two actual writing projects, you will find these steps less awkward and much easier to take. Indeed, as you become familiar with your own strengths and weaknesses, and with your own work habits, you will find yourself moving swiftly through some steps and, as you continue to pick up speed and to gain experience, even combining steps along the way.

Alas, we can't be there to answer questions while you work. But to help you get started, we have pulled together this series of questions and answers:

When I write, I just can't sit still long enough to go through all the steps you've outlined. I lose my concentration too quickly. What do I do about this?

You have hit upon a key point about the writing process: it is exhausting, both physically and mentally. You should expect to run out of gas from time to time as you work your way through the various steps. Sometimes you will be able to work your way through several steps before your concentration falters. Other times one single step will be so difficult, so downright tiring, that completing this one step will be as much as you can do.

There is absolutely no way to prevent an attack of "writer's fatigue". It's like the flu; when it hits, it hits. With experience you will learn to recognize the signs of a coming attack: your concentration begins to flag, you lose your mental focus and for a moment can't remember what point you were trying to make, you find yourself writing something that is so silly, so utterly useless that you can't believe you just wrote it. As we say, there is no way to prevent an attack of "writer's fatigue." However there is a cure: you do absolutely nothing except relax, accept the fact that you need to stop for a while, and you go do something else — anything else—until you are ready and able to start work again. For short pieces of writing, a five-minute or ten-minute break usually does the trick. For longer pieces of writing, you will need an hour or two. Indeed, it is quite common for professional writers to knock off work for the day when "writer's fatigue" strikes, even if it's late morning or early afternoon (provided some good work has been done). For really lengthy, complex pieces of writing—books, theses, major analytic or technical essays—it can take days or even weeks for "writer's fatigue" to pass.

Our advice is this: When you feel an attack of "writer's fatigue" coming on, don't fight it. Accept the attack for what it is, and take a break. In the long run you will actually save time, since if you try to keep working through an attack you will write such garbage, and even spoil whatever good material you had already written, that it will take more time to untangle the mess than it will to make up for lost time. Second, anticipate these attacks; they happen to everyone now and then. So as you set about your project and plan your work schedule, leave some room for "downtime."

Finally, when the attack comes do whatever works for you to put your writing project out of mind—work on some other task, return some telephone calls, listen to music, go to a movie, whatever. Just remember that taking a break to clear the cobwebs out of your brain and to re-charge your batteries is part and parcel of the writing process. So don't feel guilty about relaxing when you think you should be "working." By the way, it often happens that when you are relaxing your brain continues to think about whatever you are writing, and just when you least expect it a good idea or phrase leaps to mind.

I understand everything you've said. But somehow I still have trouble getting started. What exactly is the absolute, first thing to do when I launch a writing project?

The absolute, first thing to do when you launch a writing project is to resist the impulse to start writing. You need to clear your mind, to settle down, and above all *you need to think.* Don't worry about wasting time; it is never a waste of time to get your thoughts in order. Who has asked you to write something? Who will read it? What purpose is the piece of writing intended to serve? To persuade? To inform? To trigger action of one sort or another? Ask yourself all these questions, and don't settle for the first answers that pop into your head. And when you feel you've got your thoughts in order, then—and only then—should you move on to the first formal step in the writing process; deciding what it is you are going to write by choosing the correct category of writing product.

Your notion of using imaginary conversations at key points in the writing process; I'm not quite clear on it. Why should we do it? What's the big advantage?

The purpose of any piece of writing, in any category, is to communicate with someone. Most people find it easier to communicate in person than on paper; to talk rather than to write. Moreover, a piece of writing succeeds only when it is pitched precisely to its intended audience—to the actual person or persons for whom it is being written. By holding an imaginary conversation with your intended reader, you push toward both objectives. First, by talking out your piece of writing you leap over the period of stiffness or even paralysis that often accompanies an effort to start writing. Second, you begin to focus sharply on your intended reader or readers; to really see him, her, or them clearly and to understand what it is they need from whatever you plan to write.

My problem is length. How long is a piece of writing supposed to be?

Everybody worries about length, and everybody is wrong. Length is a non-problem. Your piece of writing — whether a thank-you note to Aunt Sally or a history of the automobile industry—should be just as long, and no longer, than it takes to say whatever you need and want to say. That, and only that, is the "correct" length for any piece of writing. Quite literally, there are no rules about length. Look in any library or bookstore, and you will find books ranging from thirty-five pages long to several volumes. We've seen business memos that were just a single paragraph, and memos that approached book length; what matters is the substance and the layout, and nothing else.

But what about the length of individual sections of a piece of writing?

Same thing. There are no rules as such, provided you keep a steady depth all the way through. Just make certain that when you get to selecting your layout, whatever you come up with is comfortable for your reader's eyes. You don't want the poor devil to go blind staring at a page of solid text, which is why on extended pieces of writing you ought to have at least two paragraphs on each page.

What's the absolute minimum length of a paragraph?

One sentence.

What's the fewest number of words you can have in a sentence?

One.

I never know how to end whatever I'm writing. What's the right way to do it?

We all know what it's like to have friends over for dinner. You finish eating, you sit around the living room for a while talking, and after you've yawned in their faces three or four times somebody finally says that maybe it's time to think about leaving. A while later everyone stands up, then half an hour later you are all standing near the door, your friends with their coats on, half asleep but still talking. It is amazing how long it takes some people to say good-bye. Likewise, it is amazing how long it takes some people to end a piece of writing. They keep going even though they've got nothing left to say.

We wrote back in Part Two that when you suddenly find yourself stuck, it's a signal that you might have the wrong outline. That is quite true. But when you suddenly find yourself stuck after you have covered all the points in your outline, it's a signal that you have reached your final destination. In this case, being stuck isn't at all a cause for concern; it's a cause for celebration. It means that you have finished the job.

But don't I need to write a summary of some sort, or have a section with all my conclusions?

Not really. You can if you want to, and if it makes you happy go ahead. But if you have written a good draft and then polished it carefully, a section that summarizes your points or your conclusions will only repeat what you have already said. Your readers are busy, so why make them plow through the same stuff twice? It just isn't necessary. In other words, don't be afraid to end your piece of writing when you have said whatever it is you meant to say. This isn't a Fourth-of-July picnic; you don't need the literary equivalent of a fireworks display so that everyone will know the festivities are over. Let your piece of writing end naturally, and it will look just fine.

You mean you don't need a special sort of ending for a piece of writing? You just let it end wherever it happens to end?

That is exactly right, and to really hammer home this point we'll do it ourselves. You see, we have told you everything we know about how to write. We can't think of a single important point to add. So we'll wish you good luck, and without making a big deal about it we'll stop right here.

How to Order More Copies

We hope you found *How to Write* useful and informative. If you know someone who would also benefit from his or her own copy—a son or daughter, nephew or niece, co-worker or business acquaintance—here's how to order:

Single Orders

Mail us a check for $8.20 ($6.95 plus $1.25 for postage and handling) and we will ship the book to the person and address you specify.

Bulk Orders

If you want to distribute copies of *How to Write* to the personnel in your organization, or if you are among the hundreds of organizations that already do so and need more copies, let us know—by mail, telephone or fax—how many copies you want and we will ship the books. Then we will send you an invoice to cover the cost of the books plus UPS shipping charges. On orders of 25 copies or more we offer a 50 percent discount—just $3.48 per copy plus shipping.

Storm King Press
P.O. Box 2089
Friday Harbor, WA 98250

Tel: 206-378-3910
FAX: 206-378-3912

Note to Instructors

How to Write is now used by instructors at colleges and universities throughout the world. It is used not only in writing courses, but in *all* courses where the need to communicate ideas and information, clearly and concisely, is deemed important by the instructor. If you wish to make *How to Write* available to your students, add this book to your required reading list, then notify your college bookstore and inform the store manager that *How to Write* is available through Publishers Group West, in Emeryville, CA: 1-800-788-3123.

How To Learn a Foreign Language

by Graham E. Fuller